THE WORLD
AMERICA MADE

THE WORLD
AMERICA MADE

ROBERT KAGAN

Alfred A. Knopf
NEW YORK 2012

THIS IS A BORZOI BOOK
PUBLISHED BY ALFRED A. KNOPF

Copyright © 2012 by Robert Kagan

All rights reserved. Published in the United States by
Alfred A. Knopf, a division of Random House, Inc.,
New York, and in Canada by Random House
of Canada Limited, Toronto.

www.aaknopf.com

Knopf, Borzoi Books, and the colophon are registered
trademarks of Random House, Inc.

Library of Congress Control Number: 2012930723

ISBN 978-0-307-96131-0

Manufactured in the United States of America
First Edition

For Tor

THE WORLD
AMERICA MADE

INTRODUCTION

IN THE FRANK CAPRA classic *It's a Wonderful Life,*
George Bailey gets a chance to see what his world would
have looked like had he never been born. It would be nice
if we could do the same for the United States, to see what
the world would have looked like had the United States
not been the preeminent power shaping it for the past six
decades, and to imagine what the world might look like
if America were to decline, as so many nowadays predict.

We take a lot for granted about the way the world looks
today—the widespread freedom, the unprecedented
global prosperity (even despite the current economic
crisis), and the absence of war among great powers. In
1941 there were only a dozen democracies in the world.
Today there are over a hundred. For four centuries prior
to 1950, global gross domestic product (GDP) rose by less
than 1 percent a year. Since 1950 it has risen by an average of 4 percent a year, and billions of people have been
lifted out of poverty. The first half of the twentieth century saw the two most destructive wars in the history of

mankind, and in prior centuries war among great powers was almost constant. But for the past sixty years no great powers have gone to war with one another. Our era is best known for the war that never happened, between the United States and the Soviet Union.[1]

There's plenty wrong with our world, of course, but from the perspective of thousands of years of recorded history, in which war, despotism, and poverty have been the norm, and peace, democracy, and prosperity the rare exceptions, our own era has been a golden age.

Some believe this is the inevitable result of human progress, a combination of advancing science and technology, an increasingly global economy, strengthening international institutions, evolving "norms" of international behavior, and the gradual but inevitable triumph of liberal democracy over other forms of government—forces of change that transcend the actions of men and nations.

But there is also another possibility. Perhaps the progress we enjoy was not an inevitable evolution of the human species but rather the product of a unique and perhaps fleeting set of circumstances: a particular arrangement of power in the international system that favors a certain worldview over others. Maybe if those conditions were to change, if power were to shift, then the characteristics of the world order would change, too. Perhaps democracy has spread to over a hundred nations since 1950 not simply because people yearn for democracy but because the most powerful nation in the world since 1950 has been a democracy. Perhaps the stunning global economic growth of the past six decades reflects an economic order shaped by the world's leading free-market economy. Perhaps the era of peace we have known has something to do with the enormous power wielded by one nation.

History shows that world orders, including our own, are transient. They rise and fall. And the institutions they erected, the beliefs that guided them, and the "norms" that shaped the relations among nations within them—they fall, too. Every international order in history has reflected the beliefs and interests of its strongest powers, and every international order has changed when power shifted to others with different beliefs and interests. On some occasions, the prevailing world order has simply collapsed into disorder. When the Roman Empire fell, the order it supported fell, too. Not just Roman government and law but an entire economic system stretching from northern Europe to North Africa was disrupted and would take centuries to rebuild. Culture, the arts, even progress in science and technology, were set back for centuries. People lost the recipe for cement.

We saw a similar collapse of world order in our own time. The world we know today was erected amid the chaos and destruction following World War II and the collapse of the European-dominated order that had evolved over four centuries. That order was far from perfect: it produced many wars, an aggressive imperialism, and the widespread oppression of nonwhite races, but it also produced the conditions for an era of great human advances. By the late nineteenth century British control of the seas and the balance of great powers on the European continent together had provided the relative security and stability to allow a growth in prosperity, a modest if tenuous expansion of personal freedoms, and a world knit closer by the revolutions in commerce and communication we today call globalization. It kept peace among the great powers for almost four decades after the Napoleonic Wars, and for another four decades after the wars of German unification. It was so successful that many concluded at the dawn of the twentieth century that mankind had reached a summit of evolution and that major war and tyranny had become obsolete.

Yet with the outbreak of World War I, the age of settled peace and advancing liberalism—of European civilization approaching its pinnacle—collapsed into an age of hyper-nationalism, despotism, and economic calamity. The once promising spread of democracy and liberalism halted and then reversed course, leaving a handful of outnumbered and besieged democracies living nervously in the shadow of their newly fascist and totalitarian neighbors. Suddenly it was a world filled with predatory leaders sitting atop predatory powers. The collapse of the British and European orders in the twentieth century did not produce a new dark age—though if Nazi Germany and imperial Japan had won the war, it might have—but the cataclysm it did produce was, in its own way, no less devastating.

Would the end of the present American order have less dire consequences? That is a question worth asking now, as so many contemplate the prospect of American decline. A surprising number of American intellectuals, politicians, and policy makers greet that prospect with equanimity. There is a general sense that the end of the era of American preeminence need not mean the end of the present liberal international order. The expectation, if not assumption, is that the good qualities of that order—the democracy, the prosperity, the peace among great powers—can transcend the decline of American power and influence. Even with diminished American power, the political scientist G. John Ikenberry writes, "the underlying foundations of the liberal international order will survive and thrive."[2] And there is an accompanying view that American decline is in any case already a fact of life, so whether it is a good thing or a bad thing, there is nothing we can do about it.

Against this backdrop, it is worth exploring to what degree the present world order depends on American power and its unique qualities. What would it mean for the future if the international order were no longer shaped primarily by the United States and like-minded allied nations? Who or what would take America's place? And there is another set of questions, equally important: Is America really in decline? Or are Americans in danger of committing preemptive superpower suicide out of a misplaced fear of declining power?

MEET GEORGE BAILEY: WHAT IS AMERICAN ABOUT THE AMERICAN WORLD ORDER?

WHY CALL IT THE "American world order" at all? The United States has certainly not shaped the international environment by itself. Many other peoples, as well as broad historical forces—the evolution of science and technology, fluctuations in the availability of natural resources, long-term economic trends, population growth—have also created today's world. Peoples on every continent have worked and suffered to lift themselves out of poverty and destruction and to make better lives for themselves and their children. The world is too big for any nation to shape by itself. Nevertheless, in any given historical period, the most powerful nations do put their own particular stamp on the international order, if only by virtue of their relative weight in the system. They establish many of the "norms" and rules of international behavior. They shape the nature of economic relations. They can even have influence in the realm of ideas and beliefs, including the way peoples worship their gods and the forms of government they consider legitimate. For many centuries the predominant power of China shaped the way millions of people throughout Asia thought, spoke, worshipped, painted, and carried on their commerce. In the nineteenth century, the great European powers imposed standards of international and domestic behavior not only for Europeans but for millions throughout Africa, Asia, and Latin America. There has been an Egyptian order, a Roman order, a Greek order, an Islamic order, a Mogul order, an Ottoman order, and many others, and historians will undoubtedly view the period from the end of World War II until some yet to be determined moment as an American order.

Yet it has also been the American order in a more specific sense. It is not just that the United States has been the most influential power in the international system. The most important features of today's world—the great spread of democracy, the prosperity, the prolonged great-power peace—have depended directly and indirectly on power and influence exercised by the United States. No other power could have or would have influenced the world the way Americans have because no other nation shares, or has ever shared, their peculiar combination of qualities.

Some of the most important qualities are obvious. America's unique geographical circumstances, its capitalist economic system, its democratic form of government, and its enormous military power have together shaped a particular kind of international order that would have looked very different had another nation with different characteristics wielded a similar amount of influence.

Less easy to grasp, but just as important to understanding the nature of the American world order, is the complex character of the American people. This is no simple paean to Americans' superior virtues. Some portray Americans as farseeing builders of international institutions and structures of liberal order, as thoughtful "operators" and "managers" of vast global systems.[3] But few Americans, and few non-Americans, would recognize this portrait. In most respects, Americans are like any other people, with a blend of selfishness and generosity. More than most, they have been a people of contradictory impulses and a most ambivalent view of what role, if any, they ought to play in the world.

They are a people rife with potent national myths that both inspire and mislead them. Start with the fact that one of the most powerful, influential, and expansive peoples in history still think of themselves as aloof, passive, self-contained, and generally inclined to minding their own business. In less than two centuries Americans

transformed their nation from a sliver of settlement cling-
ing to a coastline into a globe-girdling superpower with
historically unparalleled power and influence. Yet to hear
Americans tell it, they are the Greta Garbo of nations:
they just want to be left alone. In their national mythol-
ogy, the two-centuries-long subjugation of the North
American continent, a region inhabited by Spaniards,
French, and Russians, as well as by an entire race of indig-
enous peoples, was not conquest but the peaceful settlement of an empty frontier. Americans do not go "abroad
in search of monsters to destroy" is the oft-quoted phrase
of John Quincy Adams. If someone points out to them
that they have, indeed, often done just that, then they
portray themselves as the "reluctant sheriff," their boots
on the desk, reading the newspaper until some unsavory
gang rides into town and forces them to pull their rifle
off its rack, whether Japanese imperialists, Nazis, Soviet
communists, or Islamic jihadis. "The United States of
America never goes to war because we want to," said one
prominent politician a few years ago. "We only go to war
because we have to."[4]

But this self-perception, while sincere, bears no relation to reality. Since the late nineteenth century, when
the United States became a world power, Americans have
used force dozens of times, and rarely because they had
no choice.[5] They have sent troops to Mexico and Central
America to depose troublesome leaders; they have fought
the Spanish in Cuba and independence-minded guerrillas
in the Philippines; they have fought anti-Western forces
in China and communists in Vietnam and Korea, and
have sent millions of troops to Europe, twice; they have

fought dictators and jihadis in the Middle East, Central Asia, and Africa. And they have done so for many reasons: to defend themselves from distant threats, to preserve economic interests, to protect peoples from slaughter, to resist aggression, to fight tyranny, to support democracy. Far more than any other democratic people in the world today, Americans see war as a legitimate, even essential, tool of foreign policy.[6] Few modern nations, and no modern democracies, more revere their military heroes, both past and present. But every time they go to war, Americans promise themselves they'll never do it again.

They are even ambivalent about the cause of democracy, with which they have always been so closely identified. Americans, even in Woodrow Wilson's day, never had a master plan for making the world over in their image. They have often ignored the dictators in their midst, allied with them, aided them, and done business with them. They are not missionaries. But neither have they been able to escape their democratic identity, their democratic conscience, and their conviction that their special cause is, as Ben Franklin said, the "cause of all mankind." To be an American is to believe in and be committed to what Americans, and only Americans, like to call "our way of life." Since they believe their founding principles are universal, they measure all other peoples against the same rigid standard. This highly ideological view of the world tells them that all nondemocratic governments are inherently illegitimate and therefore transient. Even John Quincy Adams, in the same speech in which he warned against seeking monsters to destroy, urged the peoples of Europe to follow the American example and mount revolutions against centuries-old monarchies: "Go thou and do likewise!"

Often Americans have done more than exhort. They have gone out to destroy the monsters, and usually much to the monsters' surprise. A century ago it was José Santos Zelaya and Victoriano Huerta. In recent years it has been Manuel Noriega, Slobodan Milosevic, Mullah Omar, Saddam Hussein, and Muammar Qaddafi who have had their rules, and in some cases their lives, ended with the help of American force. Yet having leaped into action against these dictators, Americans have often been plagued by doubt. They have resented the costs, both material and moral. Wars are expensive, and occupations even more so. They have also repeatedly rediscovered the unavoidable ethical quandaries of exercising power. Liberating a people requires the same brutal force as conquering them. Even moral wars have immoral consequences. Neither people nor nations can use the tools of war and coercion and hope to keep their hands clean.

Americans have never been comfortable with these brutal facts of life. Their founding ideology contains an irresolvable tension between universalism, the belief that every human being must be allowed to exercise his or her individual rights, and individualism, the belief that among those rights is the right to be left alone. This has made them ambivalent and suspicious about power, even their own, and this ambivalence is often paralyzing. No sooner do they invade and occupy a country than they begin looking for the exits. Critics point out how inferior to the British Empire they are in this respect, but the British for centuries had few if any moral qualms about ruling other peoples. They believed they had a vocation to rule. They maintained a professional imperial service and a permanent colonial office. Americans may be "imperialists" in the eyes of many, but if so, they are reluctant, conscience-ridden, distracted, halfhearted imperialists. They did not want colonies, even the ones they seized and held for decades. They have no trained cadres for rebuilding and managing the nations they invade and occupy. To give themselves such capabilities would be to acknowledge that they are actually in the business of foreign intervention and occupation. Americans will station forces overseas for decades, so long as no one tells them in advance that that is what they are going to do.[7] But they have never considered themselves more than temporarily involved in the management of others' affairs, even as they have kept troops in some foreign lands for a half century or more.

Given all this, it is hardly surprising that Americans have been ambivalent about their role as global leader. When first challenged to take on that responsibility after World War I, a majority of Americans balked. Only after World War II, with some shame and misgiving for their global abstention in the 1930s, did they grudgingly accept an unusual share of responsibility for the state of the world. But it was a frightening and, at first, unwelcome burden, shouldered not out of magnanimity but only in response to a perceived threat from the Soviet Union. Harry Truman spoke for many when he declared it "the most terrible responsibility that any nation ever faced."[8]

Yet, for all their misgivings, most Americans have also developed a degree of satisfaction in their special role.

During the seventh-inning stretch in every game at Yankee Stadium, the fans rise and offer "a moment of silent prayer for the men and women who are stationed around the globe" defending freedom and "our way of life." A tribute to those serving, yes, but with an unmistakable glint of pride in the nation's role "around the globe."

"We are Americans: part of something larger than ourselves," declared George H. W. Bush on the eve of the first Gulf War. "For two centuries we've done the hard work of freedom." Even today, presidents and politicians speak of the "leader of the free world" (Barack Obama), the "indispensable nation" (Madeleine Albright) upon which "the world is counting" for "global leadership" (Hillary Clinton). Of course, no sooner are these words uttered than the pride fades and the concerns rise, and the same leaders start talking about the need to focus on "nation building at home."

Americans, in foreign policy, are torn to the point of schizophrenia. They are reluctant, then aggressive; asleep at the switch, then quick on the trigger; indifferent, then obsessed, then indifferent again. They act out of a sense of responsibility and then resent and fear the burden of responsibility they have taken on themselves. Their effect on the world, not surprisingly, is often the opposite of what they intend. Americans say they want stability in the international system, but they are often the greatest disrupters of stability. They extol the virtues of international laws and institutions but then violate and ignore them with barely a second thought. They are a revolutionary power but think they are a status quo power. They want to be left alone but can't seem to leave anyone else alone.

They are continually surprising the world with their behavior, but not nearly as much as they are continually surprising themselves.

When Winston Churchill observed that Americans could always be counted on to do the right thing, but only after exhausting all other alternatives, it was a sardonic, backhanded kind of compliment. Over the course of the first half of the twentieth century he watched them try to do the wrong thing many times. He watched them stay out of World War I in Europe until it was almost too late to prevent a German victory. In the interwar years, he saw them reject participation in the League of Nations and then waited anxiously for them to abandon neutrality and throw their weight against Hitler, which they did only after the attack on Pearl Harbor and only when it was almost too late again. At the dawn of the Cold War he found them insufficiently attentive to the threat of the Soviet Union; then he found them too uncompromising. He knew Americans when they were "sunk in selfishness," and yet he marveled "at America's altruism, her sublime disinterestedness." He compared the United States to some "gigantic boiler," quiet and cold until "the fire is lighted under it," and then with "no limit to the power it can generate."[9] Above all, he knew Americans were human beings, neither devils nor angels.

THAT IS IMPORTANT TO keep in mind. It is nations, made up of people, that shape the world, not gods or angels. That is why the present order, shaped by Americans, often unconsciously, and with all their peculiarities and flaws, is all the more remarkable. The great master-mind of Germany's unification, Otto von Bismarck, is supposed to have said that God looks out for drunkards, fools, and the United States of America. Perhaps that extends to the world order that Americans have built and maintained, almost despite themselves.

THE WORLD AMERICA MADE

THE IRONY IS THAT the peculiar blend of qualities that Americans have displayed, not all of them admirable, not all of them noble, and not all of them obvious traits of effective leadership, have nevertheless been a strange kind of asset to American foreign policy. For while it is true that the United States has been a powerful if unpredictable and often unwitting agent of change in the world, the ambivalence of the American people as well as their lack of self-awareness has paradoxically made their awesome power less threatening than it might be. Americans would be scarier if they actually had a plan. Their very distractedness, their evident desire to hold themselves apart from the world even as they shape it with their power, makes them an often frustrating ally, a confusing adversary, but also a less imposing, less frightening hegemon.

These qualities proved indispensable more than six decades ago when the United States laid the main foundation for today's liberal world order by cementing its economic and strategic alliance with Europe. It is easy to forget, now that Europe is supposedly passé and we've entered the "Asian century," that the world we know today—the political, economic, and strategic order in which Asia itself has prospered—was born atop the rubble of Europe after World War II. And it was born only because the United States supplied a novel solution to Europe's insoluble problem.

The European powers after the mid-nineteenth century had fallen into a tragic syndrome from which they were unable to extricate themselves. Too many strong and ambitious powers were too close to one another to offer any of them a measure of security. The European balance of power had worked for stretches of time, but it had also failed periodically and catastrophically. Between 1850 and 1945, France and Germany (or Prussia in the first instance) went to war three times—in 1870, 1914, and 1940. Russia and Germany went to war twice. Britain and France together fought Russia once. In between these major wars were several near wars as tensions rose, especially in the Balkans but also in the division of colonial spoils in Africa and East Asia. Even when the European balance of power succeeded in keeping the peace, it was through the constant threat of war, the dispatch of battle fleets to contested waters, the menacing mobilization of ground forces during crises. Europe had become a cockpit of geopolitical rivalry between heavily armed great powers, with no way of ending the cycle of insecurity. All this had transpired despite a common European culture and civilization, an increasingly integrated and interdependent European economy, and blood relations among some of the ruling families.

Enter the United States, reluctantly. Even after World

War II most Americans had never intended to become a global power. Preserving world peace, most imagined vaguely, would somehow be the job of the United Nations. When war ended, the Truman administration looked to pull back across the ocean, rapidly demobilize its armed forces, cut the defense budget, and establish Europe as an independent "third force," capable of standing up to the Soviet Union by itself. That was the original aim of the Marshall Plan and other efforts to boost Europeans' shattered confidence, rebuild their devastated economies, and turn onetime enemies into a united European entity. The Europeans, however, were not interested in being a third force, nor, as quickly became apparent, were they capable of it on their own. They wanted "American troops" standing "between them and the Red Army" and to keep a revived Germany in check.[10] The NATO alliance was really Europe's idea more than America's, an "invitation to empire," which the Americans grudgingly accepted only when it became clear their original plan was hopeless.[11]

George Kennan opposed the idea of NATO or any extended American presence in Europe. He feared Americans were "not fitted, either institutionally or temperamentally, to be an imperial power in the grand manner," and he much preferred to divest "ourselves gradually of the basic responsibility for the security of western Europe."[12] Yet it was precisely Americans' limitations and hesitations that made them such an attractive leader of the transatlantic "empire." With the Soviet version of empire taking hold in the East, the great power across the ocean, distant both physically and emotionally, appeared to Europeans as the perfect deus ex machina to solve their dilemma. The United States was geographically far enough away to be a less threatening hegemon, and with no enemies on its own borders, it was secure enough at home to keep large numbers of its powerful armed forces on permanent station thousands of miles away. It helped that America was a democracy, not only because Americans shared common values with the British and the French, but also because, as the historian John Lewis Gaddis has noted, their style of working with allies had a democratic quality that permitted weaker powers a very unimperial autonomy.[13]

The United States played a similarly critical role in East Asia after World War II. There, too, large-scale war among neighboring powers had become common by the end of the nineteenth century. Japan and China fought each other several times between 1895 and 1945, at a cost of tens of millions of lives, mostly Chinese. Japan and Russia fought each other twice. Korea served as the battleground for a number of conflicts, and of course the civil war in Korea sucked in both the United States and China. The entrance of the United States into a permanent security role in the region did not put an end to war—the United States itself fought in both Korea and Vietnam—but it did put an end to the cycle of warfare among the region's great powers. The close American security relationship with Japan mirrored the role the United States played in Germany. The region's most aggressive power was put out of the aggression business, its people's vast energies channeled instead into economic growth, technological innovation, and world trade.

It is worth reflecting on these great geopolitical problems that the United States solved after 1945, for had they not been solved, the world would look entirely different today. The strategic relationships Americans formed in Europe and Asia became the pillars of the liberal world order during the Cold War, the engines of the global economy, the heart of the expanding democratic world, and the primary guarantee against world wars and the great-power conflicts that had plagued the world for a century. Over time the self-contained liberal order built around American leadership during the Cold War proved too strong, economically, militarily, and politically, for its chief competitor, the Soviet Union, and its own efforts to establish a global communist order. The American order became the dominant world order. Moscow's former satellites eagerly joined "the West," thereby making possible the full flowering of the liberal world that we enjoy today.

THERE WAS NOTHING INEVITABLE about this turn of events. No divine providence or progressive teleology, no unfolding Hegelian dialectic required that liberalism triumph after World War II. Those who live in this remarkable world tend to assume that both the global explosion of democracy and the liberal economic order of free trade and free markets that have spread prosperity these past sixty years were simply a natural stage in humankind's upward progress. We like to believe that the triumph of democracy is the triumph of an idea and the victory of market capitalism is the victory of a better system, and that both are irreversible.

It's a pleasant thought, but history tells a different story. Democratic progress and liberal economics have been and can be reversed and undone. The ancient democracies in Greece and the republics of Rome and Venice all fell to more powerful forces or through their own failings. The evolving liberal economic order of the late nineteenth and early twentieth centuries collapsed in the 1920s and 1930s. The better idea doesn't have to win just because it is a better idea. It requires great powers to champion it.

Consider the ups and downs of democracy in just the last two centuries. From the time of the American Revolution until near the end of the nineteenth century, there had never been more than five nations in the world that could be called democracies. A brief flurry of liberal and constitutional revolutions in Europe in 1848 had been suppressed. But in the late nineteenth century there was an upswing. By 1900 there were a dozen democracies in the world, a growth so astonishing that contemporaries believed a democratic revolution was about to sweep the planet. Then came World War I and the victory of Great Britain, France, and the United States. Democratic governments sprouted up all across Europe, in the defeated powers of Germany, Austria, and Ottoman Turkey, in Finland, Poland, and Greece, and then also in Latin America. In 1920, with the number of democracies suddenly doubled, the historian James Bryce wondered, along with many others, whether this "trend toward democracy" was no temporary fluctuation but "a natural trend, due to a general law of social progress."[14] As the British economist J. A. Hobson later recalled, democracy "was making such advances in most countries of the world as to be considered the natural goal of political evolution. Even those who distrusted it believed it to be inevitable."[15]

Over the course of the 1920s and 1930s, however, the trend moved in the other direction—a "reverse wave," as Samuel P. Huntington called it. It began with Mussolini's fascist takeover in Italy in 1922. Then the newly born democracies in Lithuania, Poland, Latvia, and Estonia fell. Then came the rise of Hitler and the Nazis in Germany in the early 1930s and their forcible takeover in Austria and then Czechoslovakia. Greek democracy fell in 1936, and Spanish democracy fell to Franco and his fascist regime that same year. Military coups overthrew democratic governments in Portugal, Brazil, Uruguay, and Argentina. Japan's democracy became a façade for military rule in the 1930s. Across three continents, fragile democracies gave way to authoritarian forces exploiting the vulnerabilities of the democratic system, while others fell prey to economic depression. There was a ripple effect, too—the success of fascism in one country strengthened similar movements elsewhere. Spanish fascists received military assistance from the fascist regimes in Germany and Italy. By 1939, on the eve of World War II, the number of democracies had fallen back to no more than a dozen. All the democratic gains of the previous forty years had been wiped out.

The period after World War I showed not only that democratic gains could be reversed but that democracy did not always have to win the competition of ideas. It wasn't just that democracy was overthrown. As Hobson observed, the very idea of democracy was "discredited."[16]

Its aura of inevitability vanished. Great numbers of people did not believe democracy was a better form of government.

The fascist governments looked stronger, more energetic and efficient, and more capable of providing reassurance in troubled times. They also appealed effectively to nationalist sentiments. The many weaknesses of Germany's Weimar democracy and of the fragile and short-lived democracies of Italy and Spain made their people susceptible to the appeals of Hitler, Mussolini, and Franco, just as the weaknesses of Russian democracy in the 1990s made a more authoritarian government under Vladimir Putin attractive to many Russians—at least for a while. It turns out that human beings yearn not only for freedom, autonomy, individuality, and recognition. Especially in times of difficulty, they also yearn for security, order, and a sense of belonging to something larger than themselves, something that submerges autonomy and individuality—which autocracies often provide better than democracies. People also tend to follow winners. In the 1920s and 1930s the democratic capitalist countries looked weak compared with the apparently vigorous fascist regimes and with Stalin's Soviet Union.

It took another war and another victory by Allied democracies (and the Soviet Union) over the fascist governments to reverse the trend again. The United States imposed democracy through force and prolonged occupations in West Germany, Italy, Japan, Austria, and South Korea. With the victory of the democracies, and the discrediting of fascism, many other countries followed suit. Greece and Turkey both moved in a democratic direction, as did Brazil, Argentina, Peru, Ecuador, Venezuela, and Colombia. Some of the new nations born as Europe shed its colonies also experimented with democratic government, the most prominent example being India. By 1950 the number of democracies had grown to between twenty and thirty, representing close to 40 percent of the world's population.

Was this the victory of an idea or the victory of arms, the product of an inevitable human evolution or, as Huntington later observed, of "historically discrete events"?[17] The evidence suggests the latter, for it turned out that even the great wave of democracy following World War II was not irreversible. Another "reverse wave" hit from the late 1950s through the early 1970s. Peru, Brazil, Argentina, Bolivia, Chile, Uruguay, Ecuador, South Korea, the Philippines, Taiwan, Pakistan, Indonesia, and Greece all fell back under authoritarian rule. In Africa, Nigeria was the most prominent of the newly decolonized nations where democracy failed. By 1975, over three dozen governments around the world had been installed by military coup.[18]

This reverse wave occurred, moreover, at a time of significant growth in global GDP. The greatest surge in the global economy occurred between 1950 and 1975, and it slowed appreciably thereafter. So while more countries were moving into the phase of economic development that political scientists consider most favorable to democracy, the number of democracies in the world actually declined. Few spoke of democracy's inevitability in the 1970s or even in the early 1980s. As late as 1984, Huntington himself believed "the limits of democratic development in the world" had been reached. He noted the "unreceptivity to democracy of several major cultural traditions" as well as "the substantial power of antidemocratic governments (particularly the Soviet Union)" as contributing to democracy's dim future.[19]

But then, unexpectedly, came the "third wave." From the late 1970s through the early 1990s the number of democracies in the world rose to an astonishing 120, representing well over half the world's population. And it is possible that in the Arab Spring we are seeing a continuation of this third wave, or perhaps even a fourth. The explosion of democracy is now about to enter a fifth straight decade, the longest and broadest such expansion in history. Although there has been backsliding in some parts of Latin America and the former Soviet Union, we have yet to witness a reverse wave.

What explains the prolonged success of democratization over the last quarter of the twentieth century? It cannot only be the steady rise of the global economy and the general yearning for freedom, autonomy, and recognition. These were critical ingredients, but they were not sufficient. Presumably, human beings always have an innate yearning for autonomy and recognition, when these are not outweighed by other concerns and innate yearnings. And the economic growth between 1950 and 1973 was even greater than in the years that followed. Yet neither human yearnings nor economic growth prevented a reversal of the democratic trend in the 1960s and early 1970s. Until the third wave, many nations around the world careened back and forth between democracy and authoritarianism, in a cyclical and almost predictable manner. What has been most notable about the third wave is that this cyclical alternation between democracy and autocracy has been interrupted. Nations have moved into a democratic phase and stayed there. But why?

The answer is related to the configuration of power and ideas in the world. The international climate from the mid-1970s onward has simply been more hospitable to democracies and more challenging to autocratic governments than in past eras. In his study, Huntington noted such factors as the change in the Catholic Church's doctrine regarding order and revolution in the Second Vatican Council, which tended to weaken the legitimacy of authoritarian governments in Catholic countries. The growing success and attractiveness of the European Community, meanwhile, had an impact on the internal policies of nations like Portugal, Greece, and Spain, which sought the economic benefits of membership in the EC and therefore felt pressure to conform to its democratic norms. These norms were increasingly becoming international norms. But they did not appear out of nowhere, or as some natural evolution of the species. As Huntington notes, "The pervasiveness of democratic norms rested in large part on the commitment to those norms of the most powerful country in the world."[20]

The United States, in fact, played a critical role in making the explosion of democracy possible. This was not because Americans pursued a consistent policy of promoting democracy around the world. They didn't. At various times throughout the Cold War, American policy often supported dictatorships as part of the battle against communism or simply out of indifference. It even permitted and at times encouraged the overthrow of democratic regimes deemed unreliable—Mossadegh in Iran in 1953, Árbenz in Guatemala in 1954, and Allende in Chile in 1973. At times American foreign policy was almost hostile to democracy. Richard Nixon regarded it as "not necessarily the best form of government for people in Asia, Africa, and Latin America."[21]

Nor, when the United States did support democracy, was it purely out of fealty to principle. Often it was for strategic reasons. Reagan officials came to believe that democratic governments might actually be *better* than autocracies at fending off communist insurgencies, for instance. And often it was a reaction to popular local demands that compelled the United States to make a choice it would otherwise have preferred not to make, between supporting an unpopular and possibly faltering dictatorship and "getting on the side of the people." Ronald Reagan would likely have preferred to support the dictatorship of Ferdinand Marcos in the 1980s had he not been confronted by Filipino "people power." In only a few cases—such as George H. W. Bush's 1989 invasion of Panama and Bill Clinton's 1994 intervention in Haiti—did the United States seek a change of regime primarily out of devotion to democratic principles.

Beginning in the mid-1970s, however, the general inclination of the United States did begin to shift toward a more critical view of dictatorship. The U.S. Congress, led by human rights advocates, began to condition or cut off American aid to authoritarian allies, which had the effect of weakening their hold on power. In the Helsinki Accords of 1975, a reference to human rights issues raised greater attention to the cause of dissidents and other opponents of dictatorship in the Eastern bloc. President Jimmy Carter focused attention on the human rights practices of the Soviet Union as well as on right-wing governments in Latin America and elsewhere. American international information services such as the Voice of America and Radio Free Europe/Radio Liberty put greater emphasis on democracy and human rights in their programming. The Reagan administration, after first trying to roll back Carter's human rights agenda, eventually embraced it and made the promotion of democracy part of its stated policy. Even during this period, American policy was far from consistent. Many allied dictatorships, especially in the Middle East, were not only tolerated but actively supported with American economic and military aid. But the net effect of the shift in American policy, joined with the efforts of Europe, was significant.

The third wave began in Portugal in 1974, where the "Carnation Revolution" put an end to a half-century-long dictatorship. As the democracy expert Larry Diamond notes, this revolution did not just happen. The United States and European democracies played a key role, making a "heavy investment . . . in support of the democratic parties."[22] Over the next decade and a half, the United States used a variety of tools, including direct military intervention, to aid democratic transitions and prevent the undermining of existing fragile democracies all across the globe. Carter threatened military action in the Dominican Republic when a long-serving president refused to give up power. Reagan's invasion of Grenada in 1983 restored a democratic government after a military coup. In the Philippines in 1986, the United States threatened military action to prevent Marcos from forcibly annulling an election he had lost. Bush's 1989 invasion of Panama brought democracy after the military strongman Manuel Noriega had annulled his nation's elections. Throughout this period, too, the United States used its influence to block military coups in Honduras, Bolivia, El Salvador, Peru, and South Korea. Elsewhere it urged presidents not to prolong their stay in office beyond constitutional limits. Altogether Huntington estimated that over the course of about a decade and a half, U.S. support had been "critical to democratization in the Dominican Republic, Grenada, El Salvador, Guatemala, Honduras, Uruguay, Peru, Ecuador, Panama, and the Philippines" and was "a contributing factor to democratization in Portugal, Chile, Poland, Korea, Bolivia, and Taiwan."[23]

Many developments both global and local helped produce the democratizing trend of the late 1970s and the 1980s, and there might have been a democratic wave even if the United States had not been so influential. The question is whether the wave would have been as large and as lasting. The stable zones of democracy in Europe and Japan proved to be powerful magnets. The liberal free-market and free-trade system increasingly outperformed the stagnating economies of the communist bloc, especially at the dawn of the information revolution. The greater activism of the United States, together with other successful democracies, helped build a broad, if not universal, consensus sympathetic to democratic forms of government and less sympathetic to authoritarian governments.

Diamond and others have noted how important

it is that these "global democratic norms" came to be "reflected in regional and international institutions and agreements as never before."[24] Those norms had an impact on the internal political processes of countries, making it harder for authoritarians to weather political and economic storms and easier for democratic movements to gain legitimacy. But "norms" are transient, too. In the 1930s the trendsetting nations were fascist dictatorships. In the 1950s and 1960s variants of socialism were in vogue. But from the 1970s until recently, the United States and a handful of other democratic powers set the fashion trend. They pushed democratic principles—some might say imposed them—and embedded them in international institutions and agreements.

Equally important was the role the United States played in preventing backsliding away from democracy where it had barely taken root. Perhaps the most significant U.S. contribution was simply to prevent military coups against fledgling democratic governments. In a sense, the United States was interfering in what might have been a natural cycle, preventing nations that might ordinarily have been "due" for an authoritarian phase from following the usual pattern. It was not that the United States was exporting democracy everywhere. More often, it played the role of catcher in the rye, preventing young democracies from falling off the cliff—in places like the Philippines, Colombia, and Panama. This helped give the third wave an exceptional breadth and durability.

Finally, there was the collapse of the Soviet Union and with it the collapse of communist governments across eastern Europe and the installation of democratic regimes. What role the United States played in hastening the collapse of the Soviet system will always be a subject of contention. Undoubtedly, it played some role, both in containing the Soviet empire militarily and in outperforming it economically and technologically. Nor was the turn to democracy throughout eastern Europe primarily America's doing. The peoples of the former Warsaw Pact nations had long yearned for liberation from the Soviet Union, which also meant liberation from communism. They wanted to join the rest of Europe, which offered an economic and social model that was even more attractive than that of the United States. That they uniformly chose democratic forms of government, however, was not simply the aspiration for freedom or comfort. It also reflected the desires of eastern and central European peoples to place themselves under the American security umbrella. The strategic, the economic, the political, and the ideological were thus inseparable. Those nations that wanted to be part of NATO, and later the European Union, knew they stood no chance if they did not present democratic credentials. These democratic transitions, which turned the third wave into a democratic tsunami, need not have occurred had the world been configured differently. The fact that a democratic, united, and prosperous western Europe was even there as a powerful magnet to its eastern neighbors was due to American actions after World War II.

The configuration of power and ideas in any international system invariably affects the form of government of nations within that system. Contrast the fate of democratic movements in the late twentieth century with that of the liberal revolutions that swept across Europe in 1848. Beginning in France, the Springtime of the Peoples, as it was known, included liberal reformers and constitutionalists, nationalists, and representatives of a rising middle class, as well as radical workers and socialists. In a matter of weeks they toppled kings and princes and shook thrones across Germany and Italy, in France and Poland, in Austria, Hungary, and Romania. In the end, however, the liberal movements failed, partly for lack of cohesion, but partly because they were forcibly crushed by the autocratic powers. The Prussian military helped defeat liberal movements in the German principalities. The Russian tsar ordered his forces into Romania and Hungary. Tens of thousands of protesters were killed in the streets of Europe. The sword was mightier than the pen.

It mattered that the more liberal powers, Britain and France, adopted a neutral posture throughout the liberal ferment, even though France's own revolution had sparked and inspired the pan-European movement. The British monarchy and aristocracy were afraid of radicalism at home. Both France and Britain were more concerned to preserve peace among the great powers than to provide assistance to fellow liberals. The preservation of the European balance among the five great powers benefited the forces of counterrevolution everywhere, and the Springtime of the Peoples was suppressed.[25] For several decades, therefore, the forces of reaction in Europe were strengthened against the forces of liberalism.

Scholars have speculated how differently Europe and the world might have evolved had the liberal revolutions of 1848 succeeded—in particular, how differently German history might have unfolded if national unification had been achieved under the auspices of a liberal, parliamentary system rather than by Bismarck, the "Iron Chancellor," who unified the nation by war using the great power of the conservative Prussian military led by the Hohenzollern dynasty. As the historian A. J. P. Taylor observed, history reached a turning point in 1848, but Germany "failed to turn."[26] Might Germans have learned a different lesson from the one Bismarck taught, that "the great questions of the age are not decided by speeches and majority decisions . . . but by blood and iron"?[27] Yet the international system of the day was not configured in such a way as to encourage liberal and democratic change. The European balance of power in the nineteenth century did not favor democracy, and so, not surprisingly, democracy did not triumph, anywhere.[28]

We can also speculate how differently today's world might have evolved but for the role of the United States in shaping an international environment favorable to democracy, and how it might evolve were the United States no longer strong enough to play that role. Democratic transitions are not inevitable, even where the conditions may be ripe. Nations may enter a transition zone—economically, socially, and politically—where the probability of moving in a democratic direction increases or decreases. But foreign influences, usually by the reigning great powers, are often catalysts that determine which direction change takes. Strong authoritarian powers willing to support conservative forces against liberal movements can undo what might otherwise have been a natural evolution to democracy, just as powerful democratic nations can help liberal forces that, left to their own devices, might have failed. In the 1980s as in the 1840s, liberal movements arose for their own reasons in different countries, but their success or failure was influenced by the balance of power at the international level. In the American era, the balance was generally favorable to democracy, which helps explain why the liberal revolutions of that later era succeeded. Had the United States not been so powerful, there would have been fewer transitions, and those that occurred might have been short-lived. It might have meant a shallower and more easily reversed third wave.[29]

The response of the United States to the recent ferment in the Arab world is a good example of how Americans may influence the trend toward democracy even without quite planning or meaning to do so. From 2004 to 2010, the United States had modestly increased pressure on Arab states to undertake mild political reforms, although the effort was halfhearted and uneven. When a Tunisian shopkeeper set himself on fire and sparked a region-wide movement, however, within weeks the United States found itself withdrawing support from longtime allies like Egypt's Hosni Mubarak and then, in an impulsive act of humanitarianism, using force to prevent Qaddafi from massacring Libyans in Benghazi. The United States had not set out to unseat these dictators but in both cases felt compelled to place itself on the side of people clamoring for their removal. Once these unexpected decisions were made, American power became a decisive factor shaping the regional and international environment in which the Arab political turmoil unfolded. In Libya, France and Britain took the lead, but neither could have pulled together international support or used force effectively without the United States. The United States did far less than it could have, but what it did do made all the difference. Had the United States been weaker, wielding no greater influence in the international system than Russia and China, it is unlikely the dictators in the region would have faced so much pressure and been compelled to give way or be overthrown.

It is ironic, but not unusual, that Americans, having helped topple dictators in the Middle East, are not sure how they feel about what may follow. The inevitable victory of Islamist parties in some Arab states will probably bring governments to power that are less accommodating to some American interests than the previous dictatorships had been. It would not be the first time. The United States helped throw out Marcos in the Philippines only to have the post-Marcos democratic government throw the United States out of its Filipino air and naval bases. In Latin America, Asia, and elsewhere, new democracies have often proved less reliable allies in some respects than the dictatorships they replaced. Nor are the dictatorships America topples always replaced by democracies. The United States withdrew support from the Shah of Iran in 1979 only to see a virulently anti-American and undemocratic Islamic theocracy take his place—an occurrence that many worry may be repeated in the current Middle Eastern turmoil.

The great spread of democratic governments has nevertheless been an essential attribute of the American world order. Whatever specific interests have been sacrificed, achieving Americans' broader interests in a more peaceful world and a more open economic system has compensated. It is demonstrably true that democracies rarely go to war with other democracies and that politically liberal regimes are more likely to favor liberal economic systems. Americans' enduring interest in a liberal world order generally transcends other, more narrow and temporary interests. The United States can lose an Egyptian ally but still gain a healthier world order. That is probably why Americans have sometimes chosen to support democratic movements, and sometimes only purportedly democratic movements, even when their immediate interests might argue against it. And it is that American predilection, the often uncalculating impulse to support those raising the banner of democracy, that has played such an important part in creating and sustaining the extraordinary levels of democratization in the present world order. Whether or not it is true, as Americans believe, that democracy is the best form of government and the only legitimate form of government for everyone everywhere, the great spread of democracy in recent decades would not have been possible without Americans believing it and sometimes acting on that belief.

A SIMILAR STORY CAN be told about the establishment of the present liberal economic order. It is a common perception today that the international free-market system is simply a natural stage in the evolution of the global economy. The forces of globalization, revolutions in communication and technology, the growing interdependence of nations and peoples, have created a system that is both inevitable and self-sustaining.

Yet history tells us that there is nothing inevitable about a liberal international economy, either. A free-market, free-trade global economy does not just come into being. It is a choice, and it is also an imposition. As the political scientist Robert Gilpin has observed, "A liberal international economy cannot come into existence and be maintained unless it has behind it the most powerful state(s) in the system."[30] Technological innovations and social trends may support and strengthen such an order, if people want it to be strengthened. But people and nations have to want it, and most particularly the nations with the greatest power—the dominant states—have to want it. Since nations rarely do anything that is fundamentally at odds with their most vital interests, the dominant powers must believe that an international liberal economic order is the best means of increasing their wealth and power.

It is conventional wisdom today that the liberal economic order is in everyone's interest and that all nations in positions of power would support it. As a historical matter, however, very nearly the opposite has been true. Few powerful nations have ever perceived their well-being as intimately tied to a liberal free-trade international economy and had the will and power to create and sustain it. Indeed, in the modern era of nation-states, there have only been two: Great Britain in the nineteenth century and the United States in the twentieth.[31] Other great and hegemonic powers of recent centuries—the sixteenth-century Ottomans and Philip II's Spain, France in the seventeenth and eighteenth centuries, nineteenth- and twentieth-century Germany, and the Soviet Union—had little if any interest in free markets, free trade, and a liberal economic order. Not surprisingly, none of these powers ever attempted to create such an order.

The global free-market economy we know today was created by British power in the nineteenth century, and when Britain faltered between the two world wars, that liberal economic order was not passed smoothly on to a new group of supporters. It collapsed. The only power that might have had the capacity, the interest, and the desire to uphold the global free-market order in the interwar years was the United States, but Americans were not interested in playing that role in the 1920s and 1930s. It was only when the United States took on the task of creating and sustaining a liberal economic order after World War II that it took hold, and then only in those parts of the world not controlled by the Soviet Union or China. The liberal economic order is a choice, not the inevitable product of evolution.

In the case of both Britain and the United States, an order dominated by free markets and free trade reflected the special characteristics and needs of two unusual powers—both advanced industrial democratic capitalist nations and both, crucially, "island" powers with dominant navies. Even Britain and the United States did not always favor a free-trade system. Britain was a mercantilist power from the seventeenth to the early nineteenth century. Both nations went through long periods of protectionism before embracing free trade. But at the height of their power—Britain in the mid-nineteenth century, the United States in the twentieth—both nations stood the most to gain from open markets and free trade. Their advanced industries were dominant. Their dynamic economies benefited from the export of goods and capital. Their powerful navies controlled the seas and dominated the trade routes, while their competitors were generally land powers that depended on them to keep the lanes open.

These two qualities, dominance of the seas and free-market capitalism, made Britain and the United States the fathers of the present globalized economy. For not only did these countries uniquely benefit from an open economic system in which they were dominant, but they also had a profound interest in the economic development of other nations and peoples. Capitalists cannot profit overseas from peoples who neither need nor can afford their goods. Both Britain and the United States had a potent, self-interested motive to aid other peoples, and even to make temporary sacrifices on their behalf, for the long-term goal of creating lucrative markets for exports and investment. This was more true for the United States even than for Great Britain, because the latter came into this phase of economic development still in possession of a vast colonial empire. The United States was, in the Marxist argot, a "neocolonialist" economy that enjoyed the advantages of dominance and access to open markets but without the burdens, costs, and limitations of actually maintaining colonies. The American solution, best employed in the Marshall Plan and in Japan, was to help the postwar economies of Europe and Asia get back on their feet. Americans "provided the public goods necessary for the functioning of efficient world markets because it was profitable for them to do so."[32]

It was convenient that Americans' economic interests blended so seamlessly with their preferred global security strategy. By resuscitating the economies of Europe and Japan, the United States strengthened both as bulwarks against the Soviet Union without an excessive commitment of American forces. It was the perfect capitalist solution to a problem that was strategic as well as economic.

The side effect of this essentially self-interested behavior was a period of unprecedented global economic growth, not only in the transatlantic West but in the developing world, too. As John Kenneth Galbraith once observed, "The experience of nations with well-being is exceedingly brief. Nearly all, throughout history, have been very poor."[33] During the period of American hegemony, the global economy produced the greatest and most prolonged era of prosperity in history. Between 1950 and 2000, annual GDP growth for the entire world was 3.9 percent, as compared with 1.6 percent between 1820 and 1950 and an estimated 0.3 percent between 1500 and 1820. This increasing prosperity was also much more widely distributed around the world than in the past. Even in the late nineteenth and early twentieth centuries, when Britain and other European colonial powers were investing and trading with their growing colonial empires, the principal beneficiaries of economic growth were the Europeans. For the peoples of India, China, and the rest of Asia during the age of British and European colonialism, growth rates were flat (0.03 between 1820 and 1870; 0.94 between 1870 and 1913; 0.9 between 1913 and 1950). After 1950, however, growth rates in Asia matched or exceeded those in Europe and the United States (5.18 between 1950 and 1973; 5.46 between 1973 and 1998).[34] Between 1980 and 2002 alone, world trade more than tripled.[35]

The result was a dramatic improvement in the economic condition of non-European peoples. As the economist Paul Collier has noted, the world at the beginning of this era of prosperity had been roughly divided between one billion rich people and five billion poor, with the great majority of the poor living outside the transatlantic world.[36] By the beginning of the twenty-first century, four billion of those poor had begun climbing their way out of poverty. This period of global prosperity has benefited an enormous number of the world's poor and produced rising economic powers like China, Brazil, Turkey, India, and South Africa in parts of the world that had once known mostly poverty. The United States was not directly responsible for this burst of economic growth. National policies undertaken by Deng Xiaoping in China and by governments in other countries, as well as the hard work and entrepreneurial skills of their peoples, created the new prosperity. But these economic successes took place within an overall environment that was favorable to such efforts, an international system of relative peace in which trade was increasingly free and secure and in which the dominant power had a selfish interest in the economic growth of other nations.

It did not have to be this way. The Soviet Union certainly had no interest in free markets, and neither did

China before its turn to market capitalism in the late 1970s. Continental powers lacking great naval capacity in general tend to favor closed markets that they can dominate with their superior land forces. The Chinese Empire effectively closed itself to foreign trade for centuries, until forcibly opened by Western powers. But even modern European land powers have frequently sought closed economic orders. That was the goal of Napoléon, with his Continental System, which aimed to bring Britain, the island power, to its knees by turning the continent of Europe into a closed trading system. It was Germany's consistent aim, from the late nineteenth century through the time of Hitler, to conquer and control territories in eastern Europe and in France from which it could extract raw materials and labor. Even imperial Japan, though an island power with a dominant navy, sought to set up a closed Asian economic zone, the so-called Greater East Asia Co-prosperity Sphere, which it could dominate and from which it could exclude other great powers.

In the years following World War II, many nations in the developing world did not choose the capitalist market model, partly because they did not believe they could compete effectively with the dominant capitalist powers. The world's growing wealth did not address the problem of rising income inequality within and between nations. On the contrary, it often exacerbated it. So the free-market, free-trade economy was not adopted willingly and gratefully everywhere. Americans, and Britons before them, might believe that the free-market, free-trade system provided developing nations with the opportunity to get richer. But as one scholar has observed, those "opportunities" nevertheless often had to be "imposed upon the reluctant partners . . . Free trade is the policy of the strong."[37]

Americans generally believe that the free market ought always to win out over any alternative simply because it is better. In fact, capitalism can also lose. It periodically discredits itself with its seemingly unavoidable cycles of boom and bust. Capitalist entrepreneurs seeking clever ways to game the system occasionally bring the system itself crashing down. In the 1920s and 1930s, many people in Europe, and even some in the United States, decided that capitalism was, as Marx predicted, doomed to destroy itself. In the 1970s era of high oil prices and stagflation, various statist models, like that of the Japanese, appeared to be more successful. Today, the sub-prime mortgage crisis and the Great Recession, combined with the financial crisis in the European Union, have again raised doubts across the world and led many to ask whether the Chinese model of heavy state involvement may be preferable.

Sometimes the better idea doesn't win even when it is obviously better. That was the lesson of the early twentieth century. The decade prior to World War I saw economic growth in Europe rise to a remarkable 5 percent a year as the naval "sole superpower" of the day, Great Britain, expanded trade and investment both on the Continent and around the world. "Globalization," spurred by two new inventions, the wireless telegraph and the ocean-going steamship, was as much a miracle to the people of the late nineteenth century as our own technologically driven globalization has been to us. And it had a similarly stimulating effect on the global economy. John Maynard Keynes called it an "economic Eldorado," and for a while, as he observed, this remarkable international economic boom was not disrupted by the "projects and politics of militarism and imperialism, of racial and cultural rivalries, of monopolies, restrictions, and exclusion."[38]

But then, suddenly, it was disrupted. First came World War I, with its tens of millions of casualties and its vast, nation-crippling expense. Then came the turn to state-dominated economies in the fascist countries and the Soviet Union. The new dictatorships that succeeded the failed democracies of the immediate postwar years adapted government-directed war economies for peacetime. The final straw came in the 1920s, with the turn away from free trade toward high-tariff protectionism among the advanced economies and the ensuing prolonged global depression. World War I and the postwar economic and trade policies destroyed the liberal economic order of Europe.

The lesson is that while technological advances, communications and transportation revolutions, and other factors may facilitate freer trade and freer markets, they neither guarantee them nor provide reliable safeguards against the will of powerful nations or against human folly. Many nations may benefit from the liberal economic order and wish to see it preserved. But as World War I demonstrated, nations have interests besides economics.

Wars among great powers, of course, have always been catalysts for international systemic change, obliterating old world orders and giving bloody birth to new ones. They also devastate global economies, reshape norms and ideologies, and transform the way people think, how they live, and what they believe. This was the effect of the Napoleonic Wars and the two world wars, which not only reshaped the international system but produced revolutions in Russia and China that just as significantly shaped the international order. Even more limited great-power conflicts can change the nature of the international system fundamentally: the Franco-Prussian War gave birth to a new, unified Germany, with all that entailed for the future of European peace; the Russo-Japanese War heralded the arrival of Japan as a great power capable of dominating East Asia, with all that entailed for the future of peace in that part of the world.

Many believe that wars among the great powers are no longer possible. The great-power peace that has characterized the era of American dominance is not a temporary respite but a new permanent condition of humankind, a next phase in the progressive advancement of the species that cannot be reversed. A democratic peace theory holds that because democracies rarely go to war with other democracies, the spread of democracy substantially limits the possibility of war. Many believe that economic interdependence also discourages war: nations that trade with one another and depend on each other's prosperity have no incentive to fight. If the main cause of war throughout history was the struggle to control territory, today many assume that possessing territory is not as important as possessing markets and technology. So why would nations fight for territory?

Some even argue that human beings have abandoned their historic proclivity for violence. They have become "socialized" to prefer peace and nonviolence. The evolutionary psychologist Steven Pinker, noting the dramatic decline in the number of deaths from war, ethnic conflict, and military coups since 1945, argues that man's traditional inhumanity to man has been driven "dramatically down." People have greater empathy for one another; they have learned that peaceful cooperation is more rewarding than conflict and competition; they place a higher value on human life.[39] With all these mutually reinforcing characteristics of the modern world, it is not surprising that political scientists have concluded that war among the leading powers is not only unlikely but "literally unthinkable."[40]

It is a seductive argument. Americans, Europeans, and other children of the Enlightenment tend to believe history has a direction, progressively upward, either in a straight line or as a product of dialectic, as the human species learns to control and shape both the natural world and human nature. The *philosophes* of the Enlightenment three centuries ago foresaw reason gradually triumphing over the animal instincts of men. In the international realm, they saw the rise of commercial republics as an eventual antidote to war. Increasing commerce among nations, they believed, would soften manners and tame humans' atavistic, violent impulses. They looked forward to the day when nations would be governed by laws and institutions based on reason.

The heyday of this way of thinking came almost exactly a century ago. "The day of nations is passing," declared progressive leaders at the dawn of the twentieth century. The "needs of commerce" were "stronger than the will of nations."[41] The British essayist Norman Angell, in his 1910 book, *The Great Illusion,* noted that the object of war had always been the conquest of territory but that in the modern, commercial era wealth rested "upon credit and commercial contract," not on control of land. War between the advanced nations would destroy both the aggressor and the victim. Even the conqueror could not benefit from decimated lands and destroyed industries. Therefore war between great powers would be the height of irrationality. In an increasingly democratic and commercial world, neither the people nor the bankers would allow it.[42]

Angell's book sold two million copies a century ago, and it was not just pacifists who found the case persuasive. Winston Churchill, as a young member of Parliament, argued that "those powers that have become interdependent upon others, interwoven by commerce with other States," would never "threaten the tranquility of the modern world." As for the Germans, "Why, they are among our very best customers, and, if anything were to happen to them, I don't know what we would do in this country for a market."[43] At the dawn of the twentieth century, even Theodore Roosevelt believed war "between the great civilized powers [had] become less and less frequent" thanks to "the increasing interdependence and complexity of international political and economic relations."[44]

There were other reasons to be hopeful then. Many believed that modern weaponry had become so destructive and modern warfare so horrible that nations would never willingly choose to fight.[45] The world's great powers were "losing the psychological impulse to war."[46] The wireless telegraph, the ocean liner, and the vast network of trains were allowing peoples of different nations to learn more about one another. Nationalism and xenophobia were giving way to a cosmopolitan consciousness. The dawn of the twentieth century also saw a blossoming of international treaties and peace conferences. Dozens of arbitration agreements were signed in which nations promised to submit disputes to tribunals rather than go to war. Peace conferences at The Hague produced treaties limiting certain kinds of weapons and methods of warfare deemed inhumane—the bombing of cities from zeppelins, for instance, and the use of mustard gas.

What gave such weight to all the arguments for a new and permanent peace was the fact that by the first decade of the twentieth century, there had been no war between great powers for almost four decades.[47] To those who recalled the nearly constant great-power warfare of previous centuries, this was an astonishingly long era of peace. Instead of viewing it as an interlude, people naturally came to see it as a permanent condition. Something had changed fundamentally. Humankind had evolved and reached a new plateau.

We now know this judgment, which seemed so sensible at the time, was mistaken. The outbreak of World War I, the most deadly and destructive war in history, a mere four years after Angell's best seller, revealed a failure of imagination on the part of an entire generation. They simply were not able to imagine that national leaders would behave irrationally, that they would sacrifice economic interests, even bankrupt their treasuries, out of a combination of ambition and fear, that they would view territory as a worthy object of war, that they would use all the horrible weapons at their disposal without a second thought—in violation of international agreements whose ink had barely dried—and that in all this they would have behind them the enthusiastic support of their people stirred by a very un-cosmopolitan nationalist pride.

Today we suffer from a similar lack of imagination. Once again the conventional wisdom is that great-power conflict is "literally unthinkable." Even the arguments are the same: economic interdependence, globalization, the irrelevance of territory, the spread of democracy, the unthinkable destructiveness of war in the nuclear age, the belief that nations and peoples have become "social-ized" to favor peace over war, that they value life more and feel greater empathy for others—all these have made great-power war irrational and therefore impossible. And, adding force to these arguments, once again, is the long peace we have enjoyed, the remarkable six decades without great-power conflict.

Yet we have less excuse than our forebears to believe that humankind has reached a new level of enlighten-ment. The optimists of the early twentieth century had not witnessed two world wars, the genocides, and the other horrors of our supposedly advanced era. They had not witnessed the rise of Nazism and fascism. We have seen it all and, in historical terms, quite recently. It was just seven decades ago that the United States was at war with imperial Japan, Nazi Germany, and fascist Italy. It was just thirty-five years ago that Henry Kissinger asked Americans to accommodate themselves to the permanent reality of Soviet power, with its thousands of nuclear warheads aimed at American and European cities and thousands of American warheads aimed at Russia. The twentieth century was the bloodiest in all history, and we are but a dozen years into the twenty-first. It is premature for us to conclude, after ten thousand years of war, that a few decades and some technological innovations would change the nature of man and the nature of international relations.

People are right to point to the spread of democracy and the free-market, free-trade economic system as important factors in the maintenance of great-power peace. Where they err is in believing these conditions are either sufficient or self-sustaining. In fact, these are more the consequence of great peace than the cause. In 1914, democracy and prosperity did not put an end to great-power war, but great-power war certainly helped put an end to them.

Pinker traces the beginning of a long-term decline in deaths from war to 1945, which just happens to be the birth date of the American world order. The coincidence eludes him, but it need not elude us. The power of the United States has been the biggest factor in the preservation of great-power peace. It has also been a major factor in the spread of democracy and in the creation and maintenance of a liberal economic order. But America's most important role has been to dampen and deter the normal tendencies of other great powers in the system to compete and jostle with one another in ways that historically have led to war.

It is hard to measure events that don't happen, to guess

what wars might have broken out had the United States not played the role it has played during the past sixty-five years. The only guide we have is history and a general understanding of the way great powers normally behave. We know, for instance, what Europe and Asia looked like before the United States entered the picture and changed the power equations in both regions. Germany after its defeat in World War I sought to rearm, to regain lost territory and lost honor, to protect itself against former enemies, and to restore itself as a great power. Japan from the late nineteenth century onward sought regional hegemony and coveted territory on the Asian mainland. But when American power was added to these equations after World War II, both nations took entirely different paths, as did the nations around them. Had the American variable been absent, the outcome would have been different.

American power also shaped Soviet behavior throughout the Cold War. The extent of the Soviet reach into Europe was determined by the disposition of military forces at the end of World War II, not by the modesty of Soviet ambitions. Soviet probes in Berlin from 1948 through 1961, had they not been met by the implicit and explicit threat of American force, would have changed the situation in Germany profoundly. The lack of Soviet aggressiveness in Europe thereafter, as well as in the Middle East and the Persian Gulf, was a response to red lines drawn by the United States and its allies. Even today, the continuing large gap in power between the United States and the other great powers tends to dampen natural competitive rivalries and deters attempts to establish regional hegemonies by force.

It's not just that American power is so overwhelming. The United States also enjoys a unique and unprecedented ability to gain international acceptance of its power. In this respect, it violates almost every theory of international relations. One might expect that other nations, faced with this colossus in their midst, would gang up on it and seek collectively to destroy it, weaken it, or at least severely curtail its ability to use its power. That is what both logic and most of history would predict. The Grand Alliance of European powers came together to resist the great power of Louis XIV's France at the end of the seventeenth century and then to resist Napoléon at the beginning of the nineteenth century; the Triple Entente of Great Britain, France, and Russia, despite a long history of enmity among them, arose in response to the growth of German power at the beginning of the twentieth century; an alliance of great powers rose to fight against Hitler; and in the Cold War an alliance of the advanced industrial democracies balanced, contained, and eventually undid the Soviet Union. Twenty-five hundred years ago, the rise of Persia sent Greek city-states to Athens for help, and then the rise of Athens sent other Greeks scurrying to Sparta. China's leaders are acutely aware of this long and consistent history, so much so that they have for two decades worked hard to amass power quietly to avoid a similar response, and with only mixed results.

Yet the United States, which has wielded even greater power relative to the rest of the world than these past would-be hegemons, has not spurred the rise of coalitions aimed at balancing against it. On the contrary, the acceleration of American military dominance in the

1980s and 1990s was accompanied by significant reductions in military capacity in both Europe and the former Soviet Union. As American power grew, almost all the other world powers reduced the size of their militaries. The United States thus also defied what international relations theorists call the "security dilemma." According to this theory, when one nation builds up its forces, even if for defensive purposes, other powers feel compelled to build up their military strength, too, in order to defend themselves. Yet in the teeth of Reagan's arms buildup, Mikhail Gorbachev sued for peace and began reducing Soviet power, and Russia dramatically disarmed in the 1990s.[48] Europe has steadily disarmed in recent decades as American military power has grown. And even China's arms buildup for most of the past twenty-five years has been driven more by the rhythms of its economic growth, by efforts to "reunite" Taiwan to the mainland, and by changing perceptions of its global interests than by the need to respond specifically to increases in American capabilities, although this has begun to change in recent years.

It is remarkable, even astonishing, that the American superpower, for all its flaws, its excesses, and its failures, has been accepted and tolerated by much of the world to such a degree. Indeed, America's great power has been more than tolerated. Other nations have abetted it, encouraged it, joined it, and, with surprising frequency, legitimated it in multilateral institutions like NATO and the UN, as well as in less formal coalitions. From a historical perspective, this is unique. Nations have always welcomed the intervention of a foreign power to aid them in their own struggles. But what the United States has often enjoyed when using force is something different: a broad acceptance even by nations with no vital interests directly at stake. The American-led war against Slobodan Milosevic in 1999 was supported by most Europeans, who believed they did have some stake in the Balkan turmoil. It was also supported by the Japanese, Australians, and others who really had no stake, whose support sprang from humanitarian concerns but also, importantly, from a general faith that the United States could be trusted to use its power for acceptable ends.

The fact is, when the United States goes to war, it rarely goes alone. In the Korean War, American forces were joined by those from the United Kingdom, Turkey, Canada, Australia, France, Greece, Colombia, Thailand, the Philippines, Belgium, New Zealand, the Netherlands, and Luxembourg. In the unpopular war in Vietnam, Americans had forces working in various capacities beside them from Australia, New Zealand, South Korea, Taiwan, the Philippines, Thailand, and Spain. And the habit persisted after the Cold War. In the first Gulf War, American troops were joined by forces from Britain, Saudi Arabia, Syria, Egypt, France, Morocco, Kuwait, Oman, Pakistan, Canada, the United Arab Emirates, Qatar, Bangladesh, Italy, Australia, the Netherlands, Niger, Sweden, Argentina, Senegal, Spain, Bahrain, Belgium, Poland, South Korea, Czechoslovakia, Greece, Denmark, New Zealand, Hungary, and Norway. Many nations were actually annoyed when the United States initially invaded Afghanistan in 2001 without inviting in the usual contingent of allies, but eventually more than forty nations took part in the effort. The expectation of this level of global support for American military intervention is so great that in the Iraq war of 2003, Americans were shocked and disturbed when *only* thirty-eight nations participated in either the invasion or the post-invasion occupation of Iraq. It was almost unbearable to find democratic allies like France and Germany withholding their endorsement.

The fact that Americans want this endorsement is in itself significant. They want it as a way of easing their consciences and reaffirming the justice of their decision to use force. Some measure of international approval gives them greater confidence that they are acting in the world's interests and not simply being selfish. It also means they won't be carrying the burden entirely by themselves. It's no surprise that Americans want this affirmation. More unusual is that other nations so often grant it. They are willing to acknowledge that the United States is indeed engaged in actions that serve the interests of others—that serve world order.

There are few historical parallels to this situation. No other nation in recent centuries has enjoyed such broad acceptance for its use of power. The closest example would be Britain's use of its navy to limit the slave trade in the 1830s, but even that was accepted only grudgingly by other naval powers, like France, which saw it as an assertion of British naval and economic hegemony. (And of course the slaveholding United States did not approve at all.) In a multipolar world of the kind that existed in the centuries prior to World War II, any exercise of power by one of the leading nations was seen as potentially threatening by others—an attempt to transform the existing delicate balance. In the American-dominated order, with its clear and unchallenged hierarchy, the exercise of American power is less threatening because it generally serves to confirm the existing imbalance.

This broad acceptance of American power should not be confused with helpless tolerance of U.S. predominance. There has been that, too. Nations have sometimes accepted American power because they have little choice. Europeans, including Britain's pro-American prime minister Margaret Thatcher, did not approve of the American intervention in Grenada in 1983, for instance, but there was nothing they could do to prevent it, so they registered their objections and let it pass. There is not much other nations can do when the United States decides to take military action without their approval, unless they are willing to constrain American power in some active way, which would require dramatically shifting their entire economies toward military spending. But most nations in the world, including the most advanced nations, simply do not feel threatened enough by America's great power, even when they find it unconstrained and reckless, to warrant major expenditures on their own military forces.

This is a new phenomenon in international affairs. Even when the United States has engaged in what others regard as unjustified and illegal military actions, this has not led to a withdrawal of general support for American power. The 2011 action in Libya was a prime example. Only a few years after the global uproar over the U.S. invasion of Iraq, and with American troops still engaged in that unpopular war, many nations, led by France and

Britain, and even the Arab states, were beseeching the United States to deploy its great military power again to unseat yet another Muslim ruler in an Arab country. So many nations supported the United States' use of force in Libya that two nations that certainly would have preferred not to see American power on display again—Russia and China—felt they had no choice but to acquiesce in the prevailing desire to have the United States once more unsheathe its sword.

One can't blame Moscow or Beijing for being unhappy and reluctant backers of American military action, in Libya and elsewhere. Neither of those two great powers has ever enjoyed similar international support for their use of force. When Russia goes to war, it goes alone, at least since World War II. There are no votes at the UN or in any other multilateral organization sanctioning Moscow's use of force. When Russia sent its troops into Georgia in 2008, even its own version of NATO, the Shanghai Cooperation Organization, would not give its blessing. When the Soviets intervened in Afghanistan in 1979, they went in without Polish or other Warsaw Pact troops beside them. Ironically, when Polish troops finally did go fight in Afghanistan a little over two decades later, it was alongside American troops.

When China intervened in Korea in 1950, it, too, went in alone. It has not used force since it began to reemerge as a great power, but would it receive international blessing if it did? Today, even as China lends a few ships to antipiracy efforts off the coast of Africa, it spurs a bit of nervousness among local powers, like India. Chinese strategists sometimes marvel at what the United States can get away with. As the strategic thinker Yan Xuetong puts it, the Americans have created "an institutionalized system of hegemony" by "establishing international norms" in accordance with American principles of behavior. Once these norms are "accepted by a majority of countries," American hegemony becomes "legitimized."[49] But what the Chinese find really upsetting is the extent of America's military alliances, for, as Yan Xuetong notes, "America has more than 50 formal military allies, while China has none."[50] This gives the United States an enormous advantage.

Other countries do enjoy international support when they use force: France and Great Britain, for instance, in Côte d'Ivoire, Sierra Leone, and Libya; Australia in East Timor. But they are not great powers and do not wield anything like the kind of military power the United States does. Moreover, they are part of the still-dominant global democratic club, which alone has been able to bestow some international legitimacy on military action. As a rule, either nations have possessed great power but enjoyed low international acceptance of its use, or they have enjoyed high international acceptance for their use of force but had relatively little of it to use. And it makes sense. Why should weaker nations encourage the strongest nations to use their power? The United States has been an anomaly in this respect. Since the end of World War II, it has held a near monopoly of legitimated military power, and it still does today.

Why has the world been so accepting of American military power? It is not because that power has been used either sparingly or unerringly or always in accord with international law or even always in consultation with allies. Some argue that the international system established by the United States after World War II was based on rules and institutions to which Americans bound themselves as well as others. According to this theory, other nations could trust the United States to abide by these rules, especially those governing the use of force, and to work within the institutions like the United Nations and NATO. This gave other nations a measure of confidence that the United States would not abuse its power.[51]

In fact, however, the United States has not always felt constrained by either laws or institutions, even those of its own creation. From the overthrow and attempted overthrow of governments in Iran, Guatemala, and Cuba, to the Vietnam War and the intervention in the Dominican Republic, to the invasion of Panama and the war over Kosovo, the United States under both Democratic and Republican presidents often defied or ignored international laws and institutions, both during the Cold War and in the two decades afterward.

Nor have Americans, though usually committed in principle to multilateralism, allowed themselves to be hemmed in very much by their allies or by institutions like the United Nations. The Founders' admonitions against "entangling alliances" have echoed down through the centuries, as has a very American suspicion of international institutions and any perceived constraint on American sovereignty. These have provided a counterpoise to American affection for international laws and institutions. The United States, moreover, as a very pow-

erful nation, has been no more willing than past powerful nations to be entirely constrained by weaker nations.
The United States did not hesitate to go to war over
Kosovo in 1999, despite failing to gain approval at the UN
Security Council, or to bomb Iraq in 1998, despite loud
objections from close democratic allies like France. Even
during the Cold War, as one scholar has noted, America's rhetorical commitment to "multilateralism generally
masked the substance of unilateralism."[52] As a general
rule, the United States has sought approval for its military actions only when confident it could get it, as when
Truman sought UN authorization for the intervention in
Korea while the Soviet Union was boycotting the Security
Council, or when George H. W. Bush sought UN authorization for the war against Iraq in 1991 at a time when
he knew the Soviet Union, weakened and on its last legs,
would be compliant. Does anyone believe Bush would
have refrained from acting had the Soviet Union disap-
proved? When he ordered the invasion of Panama in 1989
to remove Manuel Noriega, he was undeterred by the fact
that the UN General Assembly condemned the action
as a violation of international law, the Organization of
American States passed a resolution deploring it, and at
the UN Security Council a draft resolution demanding
the immediate withdrawal of American forces had to be
vetoed.

This sometimes cavalier attitude toward allies and
institutions has been apparent on economic matters, too.
When Richard Nixon took the United States off the gold
standard in 1971, thus putting an end to the Bretton Woods
system the United States had devised after World War II,

he did so without even consulting America's closest allies. It is hard to believe the rest of the world has regarded the United States as consistently abiding by the rules of the international system it helped devise. Although Americans would claim otherwise, and although they are among the most legalistic people in the world, the order they have sustained has never been based strictly on law, but rather on Americans' perception of their interests and on their judgments about right and wrong.

So why has the world been so accepting? The perception of American motives and goals is one answer. Whatever other countries may say, many implicitly accept that when America uses force, it is rarely in pursuit of narrow interests alone but also in defense of principles of an order that other liberal nations share and from which they benefit. In effect, many nations do agree with American definitions of right and wrong, even if they sometimes decry American methods of adjudicating. Nor can other nations fail to see the ambivalence with which Americans wield their power. It is Americans' evident reluctance to wield power, their obvious aversion to the responsibilities of ruling others—more than their commitment to laws and institutions—that makes the United States for many nations a tolerable if often misguided hegemon.

Some of this acceptance has nothing to do with what Americans say or believe or how they behave. It is simply a matter of geography—the fact that even in this modern world of rapid communications and transportation, the United States is, in geopolitical terms, a distant island, far from the centers of great-power competition. The world's cockpits of conflict for centuries have been in Europe,

Asia, and the Middle East, where multiple powers share common neighborhoods, jostle for primacy, and have engaged in endless cycles of military competition and warfare. The United States, alone of the world's great powers, is not part of such a region. It is neighbor to no other great power (with apologies to Mexico and Canada). It stands apart. No matter how deeply involved it becomes in other heavily contested areas of the world, it remains distant from them, both physically and spiritually. As a result, Asians, Europeans, and the peoples of the Middle East have invariably worried more about what neighboring powers are up to than about the distant American power, despite its far greater strength. And when the power and behavior of one of their neighbors has grown menacing, they have looked to the United States as a natural partner—comforting both for its strength and for its distance. France and Britain have turned to the United States for help against Germany; Germany has turned to the United States for help against the Soviet Union, as has China; China and Korea have turned for help against Japan; Japan turns for help against China; the Gulf Arab states turn for help against Iran or Iraq—and always because the neighboring threat looks more menacing and because the United States really has the power to help.[53]

This points to the final reason why American power has been tolerated and even welcomed by many nations around the world. They need it—or at least they feel they may need it in the future. They have accepted America's great power not primarily out of affection or admiration but out of self-interest. They have wanted the United States to be militarily powerful and also militarily engaged, even if that has meant tolerating what many regard as profligate use of that military power. In the 1960s, as German students protested in the streets against American escalation of the war in Vietnam, the German chancellor signaled caution. The United States was "fighting there for reasons of treaties and solemn obligations," he noted, and if the Americans abandoned their ally in South Vietnam, Germans might be abandoned someday, too. "It came down unavoidably to the question if one could generally trust America."[54] In 1968, criticism of the Vietnam War became temporarily muted after the Soviet invasion of Czechoslovakia. Whatever their qualms, and there have been many, America's allies would not have valued the United States as much were it not both capable and willing to use force.

This general acceptance of American power over the past several decades has been critical to the maintenance of peace among great powers. Would-be challengers to the international order, even would-be challengers to the regional orders in Asia, Europe, and the Middle East, have had to weigh not only the fact of America's lethal military but also the support it enjoys from the majority of the world's most important nations. In addition to facing American military might, a regional challenger could find itself diplomatically isolated and subject to economic and other sanctions in an international system in which the United States has much greater influence than the challenging power does.

This has certainly been a major preoccupation of Chinese leaders, especially since the events in Tiananmen Square, when the United States organized a regime of international isolation and economic sanctions targeted at the Beijing government. It revealed, in the words of Chinese scholars, the existence of an "international hierarchy dominated by the United States and its democratic allies." There was a "U.S.-centered great power group," from which China was an "outlier."[55] Were China to engage in some military action, even in its own neighborhood, not only would it have to worry about American forces and those of local powers, but it could well find itself confronted diplomatically and economically by a U.S.-led global coalition of advanced and wealthy democracies.

As it is, Chinese leaders look around and perceive an American-built wall of containment. As Hu Jintao put it only a few years ago, the United States has "strengthened its military deployments in the Asia-Pacific region, strengthened the US-Japan military alliance, strengthened strategic cooperation with India, improved relations with Vietnam, inveigled Pakistan, established a pro-American government in Afghanistan, increased arms sales to Taiwan, and so on. They have extended outposts and placed pressure points on us from the east, south, and west."[56] Chinese leaders harbor a "constant fear of being singled out and targeted by the leading powers, especially the United States," and a "profound concern for the regime's survival, bordering on a sense of being under siege."[57] The prospect of this global American *posse comitatus,* together with the hard reality of American military power, has been something to take seriously. As careful students of history, the Chinese are well aware of the fates of Germany, Japan, and the Soviet Union.

The unusual combination of vast power and remarkable global acceptance of that power is the main factor that has deterred great-power war. We are dazzled by democratization, globalization, and interdependence, and believe these are the new developments that have made our world so different. But these trends have been ebbing and flowing for more than a century, and they have not prevented catastrophic wars in the past and cannot be relied upon in the future. The much-vaunted democratic peace theory would be more persuasive if the great powers were, in fact, all democracies. It could explain why Germany and France have not gone to war, but it does not explain why China and Russia, two great-power autocracies, have yet to become involved in conflicts with other great powers. Economic interdependence did not prevent two world wars in the twentieth century, and even today great powers cannot be relied upon to base all decisions of peace and war on economic considerations. One could imagine China attacking an independence-minded Taiwan despite the possible economic consequences. The American wars in Iraq and Afghanistan have not exactly been a boon to the American economy. Neither men nor nations live by bread alone. Nationalism, honor, fear, and other human emotions, as well as calculations of power, shape the behavior of nations just as they shape the behavior of the people who inhabit nations.

The common view that there can be no wars for territory, because territory no longer matters in this digitalized age of economic interdependence, is also questionable. One only has to look at the military deployments of nations like China, Russia, India, and Pakistan to see that,

to them, territory matters very much indeed. China insists
that restoring and preserving its "territorial integrity"—
including Tibet, Hong Kong, and Taiwan—are a "core
interest," as is control of the mineral resources and shipping lanes of the South China Sea. Wars have been fought,
and could be fought again, over the disputed border
between India and China at Arunachal Pradesh, between
India and Pakistan in Kashmir, and over the territorial
boundaries of Georgia. Russian claims to the Crimea in
Ukraine and in the Arctic will likely be subjects of dispute
in the future. The question of an independent Kurdistan
embroils Iraq, Turkey, and Syria in territorial disputes.
And of course there is the territorial dispute between
Israel and Palestine, which has led to four wars in the past
and may do so again.

Can we place our faith in nuclear weapons to keep the
peace among great powers? There are those who think
so, and some have even suggested arming all nations in
the world with nuclear weapons as a way of guarantee-
ing world peace. But the "nuclear peace" would seem
even less reliable than the "democratic peace." It is possible to imagine two nuclear powers fighting a strictly
conventional war. In fact, it is precisely such a war that
both China and the United States are spending hundreds
of billions of dollars preparing for. India and Pakistan
daily prepare for conventional war over Kashmir, despite
their nuclear arsenals. In the seventeenth, eighteenth, and
nineteenth centuries, great powers fought many limited
wars for limited ends without seeking each other's annihi-
lation. Nor is the horror of nuclear weapons a sufficiently
reliable guarantee against their use. During the Cold War

world leaders spoke more often about the possibility of nuclear war than we may care to remember. The revered George C. Marshall spoke of how important it was that the Soviets understand "that the United States would really use the atomic bomb against them in the event of war."[58] Near the end of the Korean War, Dwight Eisenhower explicitly warned the Chinese that he would not be "limited by any world-wide gentleman's agreement" regarding the use of nuclear weapons, and he commented to his own advisers that a large concentration of Chinese troops made "a good target for this type of weapon."[59] Kennedy contemplated the prospect of nuclear war during the Berlin crisis of 1961 and in the Cuban missile crisis the following year. And these were just the American leaders. Khrushchev and Mao often spoke of nuclear war as but a more extreme version of conventional war.

The point is not that these factors are irrelevant to peace. They all contribute in some way to hindering the great powers from going to war. But would they be reliable in the absence of American predominance, or would they prove just as helpless in preventing war as they were in 1914? The best way of measuring whether we have reached a new era of peace is the behavior of nations. If it were really the case that nations and peoples had become "socialized" to love peace and hate war, then the nations of the world would be systematically disarming. But they are not. Only Europe is disarming. The United States, China, India, Russia, and Japan, as well as numerous lesser powers, including Brazil, Iran, and Turkey, are still willing to pay large amounts of money to prepare themselves for war. What deters them from using those weapons against one another is not conscience or commerce but a distribution of power in the world that makes success highly unlikely. Were that distribution of power to change, were there to be a genuine shift in the balance of power toward greater equality, then these great and rising powers might pursue more ambitious policies because war would be a more viable option.

The period of peace we have enjoyed is only two decades longer than that which lasted from 1871 to 1914. The extra twenty years is not enough for us to conclude that we have departed from human history into a new era of permanent peace. Instead, we must look to the special circumstances that make peace possible, factors that might easily change and produce a breakdown of peace, as has happened so frequently throughout history.

WHAT COMES NEXT?

IF AMERICAN POWER WERE to decline, what would that mean for the international order? The answer depends on what configuration of power is likely to follow American decline. Probably no single power would replace the United States as a sole superpower; the world has known only two unipolar eras in more than two thousand years. There is a somewhat greater probability of a return to a bipolar world, but it seems unlikely in the near term. The leading candidate to catch up with the United States and become a second superpower is China. Already there are Americans and Chinese who speak of a "G-2" world in which Washington and Beijing together call the shots for everyone else. The vast size of the Chinese economy will give it increasing weight in the world; some analysts predict it will dominate the world economy in the next couple of decades. But it will be more problematic for China to become a superpower in a geostrategic sense. That would require something like the collapse of all the other powers in Asia, including India and Japan, and their subservience to Beijing. This would be the equivalent of Moscow's domination of eastern Europe, but much harder to achieve. The Soviet Union wound up dominating eastern Europe because its troops were already in place following the defeat of Germany. China would have to bend its neighbors to its will either without force or through costly war. If it does not, and remains surrounded by these wary great powers, it is hard to see China wielding the kind of global power the Soviet Union did. Even the Soviet Union was not a global superpower in the way the United States was and is, partly because unlike the United States it was surrounded by other great powers.

That is why when most people think of a post-American world, they think of a return to multipolarity—an international configuration of power where several powers exist in rough parity. The United States might remain the strongest, a first among equals, but in a genuinely multipolar world its power and influence would not be dramatically greater than those of, say, China or India, while in a second tier the European Union, Russia, Japan, Brazil, and Turkey would round out the great-power club. This would be a world much like nineteenth-century Europe, where Britain was the strongest power in some respects, but other nations—Germany, France, and Russia—were also powerful and in some areas were more powerful.

What would be the effect of this shift away from American predominance to a world of rough equality among great powers? Foreign policy intellectuals who herald a "post-American" world, whether it is multipolar or, as some argue, "nonpolar," imagine that the liberal world order would still persist in roughly its current form. Many assume that a different configuration of power in the international system need not produce a less liberal and open order than the one fashioned during the era of American predominance. The world would remain largely democratic. The free-trade, free-market economic order would survive. And great-power peace would persist. The United States would have to get used to a more equal partnership with other great powers, but there is no reason why the world could not move to a new arrangement—a new "Concert of Powers," much like the Concert of Europe that kept the peace in the decades following the Napoleonic Wars. Wouldn't all the great powers have a stake in preserving the present order?

This is a very optimistic set of assumptions. For one thing, as a purely historical matter, the transition from one configuration of power to another has rarely gone smoothly and peacefully. The most recent example is the transition from the European-dominated order of the nineteenth century, which collapsed in two world wars. A more hopeful example was the peaceful end of the Cold War, but which power wants to play the role of the

Soviet Union in that scenario? The Soviet decline was not smooth but, from Moscow's point of view, catastrophic. Whatever there was of a Soviet world order was completely obliterated.

As for the assumption that all the great powers in a post-American world would share a stake in preserving the present order, that seems both questionable and, in one respect, beside the point. There are significant aspects of the present international order that some of the great powers would not be committed to preserving. And even on those aspects they did wish to preserve, the question is, could they?

One element of the triad of the present liberal international order that the great powers would not all support is democracy. Two of the great powers, China and Russia, are ruled by autocrats who show no interest in relinquishing power or opening their systems to the point of allowing free selection of leadership. Vladimir Putin has made his views on democracy clear, and all experts on China agree that the present regime's survival is the highest priority of the rulers in Beijing. While that survival may require greater economic openness, they are determined to prevent a political opening that could lead to their ouster. For both Russia and China, as for all nations, these domestic concerns shape their foreign policy. When dictatorships fell in Georgia, Ukraine, and Kyrgyzstan between 2003 and 2006, in the so-called Color Revolutions, the democratic West hailed the triumph of liberalism. But there were no cheers in Moscow and Beijing, only concern that they might be the next victims of democratic pressure. More recently, while the democratic world celebrated the Jasmine Revolution in Tunisia and the Arab Spring that followed throughout the Middle East, a panicky Chinese leadership blocked the words "Jasmine" and "Arab Spring" from China's Internet. The Russian government drafted a United Nations convention prohibiting the use of the Internet for "psychological campaigns" aimed at "destabilizing society." For the past decade both autocracies have done their best to block or at least slow down efforts by the United States and Europe to put pressure on dictatorships in Sudan, Zimbabwe, Libya, Syria, Iran, Venezuela, Burma, and North Korea—and in some cases successfully.

This is hardly surprising: autocracies aren't in the business of helping democracies overthrow other autocracies. But we should be clear about what this would mean for a genuinely "post-American" world in which autocracies and democracies wielded roughly equal power. Instead of a balance of international power that favors democracy, as has existed for several decades, there would be a more even balance, with inevitable implications for smaller nations in political transition around the world. As Larry Diamond observes, "Support from an external authoritarian power can insulate a dictatorship that might otherwise be susceptible to Western leverage, as with China's role in sustaining dictatorships in Burma and North Korea against extensive Western sanctions and Russia's obstruction of democratic pressures on regimes in Belarus, Armenia, and Central Asia."[60] This is true even today, in a world dominated by democracies. So imagine a world in which the autocratic powers were stronger and the democratic powers weaker. The shift in the rough balance of power between autocracies and democracies might be enough to tip the world into a "reverse wave," which, based on past experience, has arguably been overdue.

The balance in a new, multipolar world might be more favorable to democracy if some of the rising democratic powers—Brazil, India, Turkey, South Africa—picked up the slack from a declining United States. Yet not all of them have the desire or the power to do it. India lives in a dangerous and not very democratic neighborhood, and Indian leaders consider support for democracy abroad a luxury they cannot and need not afford. South Africa, which supported Qaddafi until the bitter end, often seems more interested in pan-African solidarity than in aiding democracy beyond its borders. Brazil, like many Latin American democracies, has veered back and forth between the often clashing principles of democracy and self-determination. Of all these rising powers, only Turkey has tentatively sought to aid democratic forces in its region, and only following more aggressive efforts by Europe and the United States. That is not enough to make up the difference. There is nothing unusual in a democracy being uninterested in supporting democratic movements beyond its borders. Asian democracies, though well established, have not been prominent in protecting or promoting democracy abroad. The United States is unusual in this respect, if not quite unique. Some European powers have made the promotion of democracy outside Europe a major goal of foreign policy, but most have not.

Indeed, in recent years the world has witnessed a

small but steady decline in the number of democracies. The Arab Spring may or may not turn the tide back again, but it is worth speculating whether there would even have been an Arab Spring in a world where the autocratic great powers, China and Russia, were relatively stronger and the United States relatively weaker. Would the Europeans have played the same pro-democratic role in the face of a stronger China's opposition, knowing that a weaker United States lacked the ability or the desire to back them up? The opening in the Arab world might have been crushed, as the movement for change in Europe was crushed in 1848. Then, too, there had been a rough balance of power between the liberal governments and the conservative autocracies, but it had not been enough to save the liberalizing movements. The British, in particular, felt constrained from supporting liberals on the Continent lest this upset stable relations with the other great autocratic powers. In a new, multipolar order, presumably, the United States would be similarly constrained.

China as a rising economic power has already put a weight on the scales in favor of authoritarianism. In Africa especially, it has provided large amounts of money to dictators in exchange for guaranteed access to raw materials. Nor should one expect it to behave differently. Russia has used its energy resources to penetrate the political systems of neighboring countries, sometimes manipulating the oil and gas spigot to support favored candidates and parties, as in Ukraine and Belarus. That is at least one reason why the former territory of the Soviet Union is one of the least democratic regions in the world. In a more evenly balanced world in which the United States had declined to a position of first among equals, both Chinese and Russian influence would be proportionally greater, with negative effects for global democracy. History shows that the distribution of world power at the top affects the course of smaller and weaker nations across the globe. When fascism was in vogue among the European great powers in the 1920s and 1930s, fascist governments began cropping up elsewhere, even in Latin America. When the Soviet Union became the world's second superpower after World War II, communist movements sprang up around the world, and leaders took up the cause of revolution. When the Soviet Union collapsed and the United States emerged as the sole superpower, the number of democracies around the world shot up. If the balance were to shift again, we can expect to see a similar change in the general trend.

What about the liberal economic order? Would it survive a redistribution of power away from the United States? Most observers assume it would. After all, they argue, all the rising powers, including the most important one, China, have benefited enormously from the economic order put in place by the United States and its allies after World War II. China has lifted itself out of poverty and is on its way to becoming the largest economy in the world in terms of overall GDP. Its economic growth is driven by exports and therefore depends on an open trading system. Its domestic development relies on access to foreign investment and foreign technology. The same holds true for Brazil, India, Turkey, and other rising economic powers. Why would any of them want to kill the goose—the liberal economic order—that lays the golden eggs?

That may be the wrong question. These powers may

not want to bring down the liberal order from which they benefit. But do they have both the will and the capacity to uphold it in the absence of predominant American power? As we have seen, liberal economic orders are not self-sustaining. Historically, their creation and survival have been the work of great powers willing and able to support open trade and free markets, and to do so using all the necessary tools, including military power, to keep avenues for trade open. Would these other nations step in to fill the gap left by declining American power?

One key element of the liberal economic order over the past two centuries has been control of the seas. Today, although we live in a digital age, goods are not beamed through the ether. Much of the world's oil and gas, raw materials, ores and minerals, and food and grain still travel by ship, which means that free trade still requires open trade routes on the high seas. Yet throughout history, shipping lanes have often become victims of international crises and conflicts, as nations have sought to control waterways and deny access to adversaries. The United States went to war twice—in 1812 and in 1917— partly in response to efforts by other great powers to blockade American trade in wartime. Since World War II, the United States has used its dominance of the oceans to keep trade routes open for everyone, even during periods of conflict. But it is not enough to have an interest in free trade. Today, Portugal and Singapore have an interest in free trade and open oceans, but they lack the capacity to keep trade routes open. Only the United States has had both the will and the ability to preserve freedom of the seas. Indeed, it has done so largely by itself, policing the world's oceans with its dominant navy with only minor assistance from other powers, while other trading nations, from Germany to Japan, from Brazil to India, from Russia to China, have been content to be "free riders." This has been one of America's most important contributions to the present liberal world order.

But what would happen if the United States ceased to carry this burden? If American decline means anything, it would have to mean an end to this hegemony on the high seas. Would today's free riders decide to take on the burdens and the expense of sustaining navies that could take over some of the tasks now handled by the Americans? And even if they did, would this actually produce an open global commons, or would it produce competition and tension? For as it happens, both China and India are increasing their naval capabilities. This has produced not greater security but a growing strategic competition between them in both the Indian Ocean and, increasingly, the South China Sea. The fact that China is trying to use its growing naval power not to open but to close international waters offers a glimpse into a future where the U.S. Navy is no longer dominant.

The move from American-dominated ocean ways to a collective policing by multiple great powers—even if it occurred—might turn out to be a formula for competition and conflict rather than a bolstering of the liberal economic order. In the nineteenth century, British naval dominance undergirded peace and global free trade, except in times of war, when Britain itself closed the avenues of trade to its enemies and their trading partners. When the world's navies became more equal—with the rise of not only the German navy but also those of Japan and the United States—both peace and the international free-trade system became imperiled. Historically, a liberal economic order has flourished under only one set of conditions—a great power with a globally dominant navy and a profound interest in a free-trade, free-market international system, the situation that existed in the latter half of the nineteenth century under British naval supremacy, and again after World War II, under American naval supremacy. The multipolar eras that preceded British supremacy and that existed between the two world wars, prior to American naval supremacy, did not give rise to liberal economic orders.

Even if one sets aside the problem of who will police the commons, it is not clear that the great powers in a new, multipolar era would be able to sustain a free-market, free-trade international system, even if they wanted to. They might kill the goose inadvertently, despite their dependence on it, simply because of the nature of their own political and economic systems.

By far the most important player in the future in this regard will be China. Its economy is projected to overtake that of the United States, at least in terms of sheer volume, at some point in this century. China's ability and willingness to support the liberal economic order will go a long way toward determining whether or not that order survives. But even optimists about China's development foresee possible problems.

Two aspects of China's economy raise doubts about whether it could or would play the role of defender of the present system. One is the fact that although the Chinese economy may become the largest in the world, it will be far from the richest. The size of its economy is a product of its enormous population, but in per capita terms China remains a relatively poor country. In 2010, China's GDP was the third largest in the world, behind the United States and the European Union. But while the United States, Germany, Japan, and other powers had a per capita GDP of over $40,000, China's per capita GDP was a little over $4,000, putting it at the same level as Angola, Algeria, and Belize. Even if optimistic forecasts are correct, by 2030 China's per capita GDP will still be only half that of the United States, putting it roughly where Slovenia and Greece are today.

This will make for a historically unique situation.[61] In the past, the largest and most dominant economies in the world have also been the richest. That was certainly true of the eras of British and American dominance. And consequences flowed from this. Nations whose peoples are such obvious winners in the relatively unfettered economic system have less temptation to pursue protectionist measures and more incentive to keep the system open. So although they are dominant, they use their dominance in such a way as to permit other nations to grow rich, too.

Chinese leaders, however, may face a different set of problems and temptations. As heads of a poorer and still developing country, they may prove less willing to open sectors of their economy. They have already begun closing some sectors to foreign competition and are likely to close others in the future. The pressure to find better-paying jobs for their people climbing out of poverty into a large lower middle class could lead them to protect certain industries that provide those jobs. A more protectionist China would be neither evil nor unprecedented. Many nations go through protectionist phases during their economic development. The United States certainly did. The problem is that China's protectionist phase could coincide with its rise to dominance of the global economy. That *would* be unprecedented. The United States was highly protectionist throughout the latter half of the nineteenth century, but as it grew to become the world's dominant economy, it gradually shed protectionism because it could make more money in an environment of free trade. Britain similarly moved from protectionism to free trade as its economy became dominant. China may be different.

Even optimists about Chinese economic and political development believe the liberal economic order will require "some insurance" against a scenario in which "China exercises its dominance by either reversing its previous policies or failing to open areas of the economy that are now highly protected." For were it to do so, "given its size, the resulting conflict could undermine the post–World War II system."[62] As the political scientist Ian Bremmer asks, "What happens when the Chinese leadership decides that its development strategy no longer depends on so much foreign investment and prefers instead to use all the tools at the state's disposal to support local companies and shelter them from foreign competition?"[63] American economic dominance was welcomed by much of the world because, by and large, like Hyman Roth in *The Godfather*, the United States always made money for its partners. Chinese economic dominance, however, may get a different reception.

A second question concerns the nature of Chinese capitalism, for it is different, too. Much of the Chinese economy, though market oriented, is dominated not by private entrepreneurs but by the government. Chinese capitalism is to a large extent state capitalism. State-owned enterprises dominate vital parts of the economy—the energy sector, for instance—and amass earnings in huge sovereign wealth funds under government control. As Bremmer notes, the purpose of state capitalism is not only to maximize profits but also to maximize "the state's power and the leadership's chances of survival."[64] China is not alone. Russia and, to a lesser extent, Brazil, Mexico, and other rising powers all practice some degree of state capitalism, especially in their control of national energy companies. But China's economy is most directed at national as opposed to corporate interests. For the China National Petroleum Corporation, for instance, profits are less important than securing long-term contracts with oil suppliers so that China need not fear a future cutoff. The company is willing to pay more for security, in the interest of the Chinese nation, than it would if driven purely by considerations of profit and the interests of the company and its shareholders. The result is, among other things, a distortion in the market that drives up prices for everyone.[65]

Whether this is good or bad, the point is that it is different. Over the past two centuries, during the eras of British and American preeminence, the leading economic powers were dominated largely by private individuals or companies. Surpluses gained from trade wound up mostly in private hands. To the degree the state benefited, or had influence over corporate decisions, it was indirect. China's system is more like the mercantilism of previous eras—Britain, France, and Spain in the sixteenth, seventeenth, and eighteenth centuries, for instance—in which governments amassed wealth in order to secure their continued rule and pay for armies and navies to compete with other dynasties and other great powers. Today, too, "China's surpluses lead to concentrated acquisition of resources in the hands of the state," which keeps the rulers in power and gives them the ability "to project power internationally."[66]

Would such a power—and China is not the only one—be a reliable supporter of a liberal economic order, or would it, as Bremmer fears, threaten "the future of the global economy"?[67] To those who insist that China would never have an interest in undermining an order in which it has prospered, the answer is that it might not be able to help it. In the fable of the scorpion and the frog, the frog nervously agrees to carry the scorpion on its back across a stream only after the scorpion insists that it has no interest in stinging the frog, since both would die. But then, halfway across the stream, the scorpion does sting the frog, and when the dying frog asks why he did it, the scorpion answers: "Because I'm a scorpion. It's my nature." China, and Russia, could end up damaging or upending the liberal economic order not because they want to but simply because it is in their nature as autocratic societies to seek above all else to preserve the state's control of wealth and the power it brings.

Even if one takes a more benign view of the role that China, Russia, and other great powers might play, and assumes that they would continue to have a stake in a liberal economic order, the question is, do they have enough of a stake? Most China experts acknowledge that Chinese rulers, preoccupied as they are with internal challenges, have so far been very reluctant to take on burdensome global responsibilities. For one thing, they do not face the situation the United States faced at the end of World War II, with one world order destroyed and another waiting to be created according to American preferences. The Chinese are being asked to take on the burden of upholding a world they did not create and that was not built with their particular interests in mind. Who can blame them for being reluctant to embrace the new and burdensome "responsibilities" that Americans and others wish to place on their shoulders? The United States found itself in similar circumstances between the wars and refused to take on those responsibilities. Today, the present order is so suited to the interests of the United States, and has been so dependent on American economic and military power, that one must wonder whether it would survive a shift to a multipolar world in which the major actor, as well as other significant players, may not be either as willing or as able to prop it up.

The challenge will be all the greater if the shift from an American-dominated world to a multipolar world leads to an increase in strategic competition and conflict among great powers. Contrary to what one often hears, multipolar systems have historically been neither particularly stable nor particularly peaceful. War among the great powers was a common, if not constant, occurrence in the long periods of multipolarity in the sixteenth, seventeenth, and eighteenth centuries, the latter culminating in the series of destructive Europe-wide wars following the French Revolution and ending with Napoléon's defeat at Waterloo in 1815.

The nineteenth century was notable for two stretches of great-power peace lasting thirty-eight years and forty-three years each. The peace was punctuated, however, by major wars among great powers: the Crimean War of 1853 and a series of wars between Prussia and its neighbors—the wars of German unification—culminating in the Franco-Prussian War of 1870–71. International relations theorists often treat these as minor disturbances in an otherwise peaceful century, but they were massive and costly. The Crimean War was a mini world war involving well over a million Russian, French, British, and Turkish troops, as well as forces from nine other nations, and produced almost half a million dead combatants and many more wounded. In the Franco-Prussian War seventeen years later, the two nations together fielded close to two million troops, of whom nearly half a million were killed or wounded. That kind of war today would not be regarded as a minor disturbance in an otherwise peaceful century.

International relations theorists look back with fondness on the European balance of power that followed the unification of Germany. Perhaps too much fondness. Yes, there was great-power peace for four decades, but the period was characterized by increasing tension and competition, numerous war scares, and massive increases in armaments on both land and sea—all culminating in the most destructive and deadly war mankind had known up to that point. Even when the balance of power was maintained, it was not only by amicable diplomacy but also by the ever-present prospect of military confrontation. As the political scientist Robert W. Tucker has observed, "Such stability and moderation as the balance brought rested ultimately on the threat or use of force. War remained the essential means for maintaining the balance of power."[68]

People imagine that American predominance will be replaced by some kind of multipolar harmony, but there is little reason to believe that a return to multipolarity in the twenty-first century would bring greater peace and stability than it did in the past. The great powers today act in a restrained fashion not because they are inherently restrained but because their ambitions are checked by a still-dominant United States. Some imagine we have entered a "nonpolar" era because, while they believe the United States is declining, they don't see other powers rising to fill regional vacuums.[69] But, in fact, other poles have not emerged, because the American world order is still intact. Were the United States genuinely to decline, great powers like China, Russia, India, and Brazil would quickly become more dominant in their respective regions, and the world would return to something like the multipolar system of nineteenth-century Europe.

The problem in such a world is less likely to come from the other democracies—though even democracies have ambitions and seek their own spheres of influence. It is more likely to come from the autocratic great powers. The democracies can be satisfied with the liberal world order the United States created, duly adjusted to suit their own growing influence. But can the autocratic powers be satisfied with a world that favors democracy and puts constant pressure on autocratic regimes?

One often hears today that the United States need not worry about China and Russia. China is a cautious actor on the world scene and is not interested in territorial expansion or conflict with its neighbors. Experts on today's Russia argue that, notwithstanding occasional neo-imperial rhetoric, the rulers in Moscow have no desire to restore the Russian Empire, to take charge of the Baltic states of Lithuania, Latvia, and Estonia, or to reunite old Soviet republics like Ukraine, Moldova, Georgia, and Belarus. But is this because they are innately uninterested in such goals, or is it because they are constrained by the global power equation from realizing these ambitions, and so temper them? There is no way to know for sure, but history suggests that when we look at the behavior of nations and try to understand their motives and ambitions, we need to be aware that their calculations are affected by what they believe they can achieve and what they believe is off-limits.

One thing we do know for sure: a China unchecked by American power would be a different China from one that must worry about American power. If Beijing today does not behave more aggressively toward Japan, or India, or the Southeast Asian nations with which it has disputes, this is not because China is inherently passive and cautious. There have been times in its history when China has taken military action, even in situations where the odds did not favor it—for instance, against American forces in Korea in 1950. Rather, it is because those powers are backed up by the power of the United States. Were American power removed from the equation, the Chinese would make a different calculation. So would those other nations. Today they are content to resist China's more ambitious designs, in the South China Sea and elsewhere, because they know the United States is there to support them. China, not surprisingly, is increasing its naval power in an effort to reduce this American role. American officials claim to be puzzled by China's naval buildup. They ask for greater "transparency" about China's intentions. They might as well ask why a tiger grows teeth. This is the normal behavior of rising great powers. It only seems unusual because the American world order has until now been suppressing these natural great-power tendencies.

The same is true of Russia and its neighbors. The continued defiance of Moscow in the Baltics, the Caucasus, and eastern Europe owes a great deal to the fact that these nations have a powerful ally to back them up. In the absence of American power, Russia would be far more tempted to compel its neighbors to accommodate Moscow's wishes, and they would be far more tempted to acquiesce. If Putin, who once called the collapse of the Soviet Union the "greatest geopolitical catastrophe" of the twentieth century, believed he could safely restore it, would he resist the temptation? He is already using every tool short of military force—energy, trade, support for politicians and parties—to bring the former Soviet states as much under Moscow's influence as possible. Nor, in the one case where he did use force, against Georgia in 2008, is it likely he would have stopped his forces short of

Tbilisi had he not been deterred by the United States and NATO.

To note this is not to impute evil motives to Chinese or Russian leaders. It is to impute normality. All great powers respond to opportunities and constraints in the international system. This includes the United States. When American power grew at the end of the nineteenth century, its global ambitions grew as well. In the twenti-eth century, the United States conducted a more active interventionist policy after the Soviet Union collapsed than it had throughout much of the Cold War. After 1989, American military interventions abroad became more frequent and occurred in parts of the world that had pre-viously been off-limits due to the Cold War standoff.

We have grown so accustomed to life in the American order that we have perhaps forgotten how nations behave as they acquire power. Increasing power changes nations. It changes their ambitions, their sense of themselves, and even their definition of their interests. It also has a way of bringing out qualities of character that may have been submerged or less visible when they were weaker. Take a friendly power, like France. Today it is a benign middling power with a fairly skillful foreign policy. Most of its Euro-pean neighbors regard it as a bit arrogant and selfish, but that is tolerable because it certainly is not dangerous. But what would France be like as a superpower? Would the character traits that people today find merely annoying or amusing become more problematic? When France *was* one of the world's two or three strongest powers, under Louis XIV in the seventeenth and early eighteenth centuries, and under Napoléon in the late eighteenth and early nineteenth centuries, it twice tried to conquer its way to European supremacy (and twice failed). Maybe a democratic French superpower of tomorrow would pursue a modest, restrained foreign policy, but if so, it would be a historical anomaly. Democratic superpowers can be ambitious, too, as the United States has amply proven. The point is that power changes nations, and sometimes dramatically. Both Germany and Japan were fairly benign as nations of moderate or little power. In the seventeenth and eighteenth centuries, "sleepy Germany" was known as a "land of poets and thinkers."[70] Prior to its modernization during the Meiji period, Japan was a hermit nation that deliberately cut off ties to the outside world and was a threat to no one. Yet both displayed a different set of qualities when they grew strong, unified, and active on the world scene.

Because shifts in relative power change national ambitions and alter constraints, a return to multipolarity would change the character of every great power's foreign policy. Those nations whose power rose in relative terms would display expanding ambitions commensurate with their new clout in the international system. They would, as in the past, demand particular spheres of influence, if only as security against the other great powers. Those whose power declined in relative terms, like the United States, would have little choice but to retrench and cede some influence in those areas. Thus China would lay claim to its sphere of influence in Asia, Russia in eastern Europe and the Caucasus. And, as in the past, their claims would overlap and conflict: India and China claim the same sphere in the Indian Ocean; Russia and Europe have overlapping spheres in the region between the Black

Sea and the Baltic. Without the United States to suppress and contain these conflicting ambitions, there would have to be complex adjustments to establish a new balance. Some of these adjustments could be made through diplomacy, as they were sometimes in the past. Other adjustments might be made through war or the threat of war, as also happened in the past. The notion that the world could make a smooth and entirely peaceful transition from the present configuration of power to a new configuration reflecting an entirely different distribution of power is wishful thinking.

One of the main causes of war throughout history has been a rough parity of power that leaves nations in doubt about who is stronger. Rough parity creates uncertainty about which power might prevail in war, which leads to a complex interaction of probes and posturing between the contending powers that greatly increase the likelihood of a genuine test to discover which is actually the more powerful. Wars tend to break out as a result of large-scale shifts in the power equation, when the upward trajectory of a rising power comes close to intersecting the downward trajectory of a declining power. The great miracle of the Cold War was that the United States and the Soviet Union never decided to test their relative strength, though there were times when they came dangerously close. There is no better recipe for great-power peace than certainty about who holds the upper hand.[71] And it is no coincidence that scholars began talking about the impossibility of great-power conflict after the Cold War, when the United States suddenly enjoyed such a vast military superiority over every other potential challenger. Were that superiority to erode, the return of great-power competition would make great-power war more likely again.

What about the famous "Concert of Europe"? Could there not be a concert of great powers to coordinate policies and preserve the peace in a post-American world? It is true that in the three-decades-long peace that followed the defeat of Napoléon in 1815, the great European powers did successfully manage their affairs and avoid war. What kept the concert working, however, was not the magic of the balance of power. It was a set of shared values, shared principles, and a shared vision on the most important questions of the day—from the shape of the European order to what constituted legitimate authority and the nature of domestic politics and society. In the immediate aftermath of the French Revolution and the destructive Europe-wide war that followed it, all the leaders of the great powers shared a common horror of radicalism and revolution. They joined together not just to keep peace but to keep a conservative peace. They wanted to make the world safe for monarchy and aristocracy. They shared a vision of a particular kind of "Europe" they wished to preserve against the challenge of liberal and revolutionary forces. That consensus soon began to fray, however, as Britain, the most liberal of the powers, increasingly objected to the insistence of its Austrian and Russian partners that all hints of liberalism on the Continent be crushed by military force. The concert effectively collapsed after liberal revolution swept Europe again in the 1840s.

People sometimes hope that a concert of great powers

might be constituted today, but do today's great powers share, as the Europeans briefly did, a vision of both international order and domestic legitimacy? Not many years ago, the answer might have seemed to be yes. In the 1990s most people believed the world had entered a period of convergence and consensus similar to that of the early nineteenth century, only this time not on behalf of conservatism, aristocracy, and monarchy but in favor of liberalism, free markets, and democracy. The 1990s were the End of History, the triumph, in the words of one scholar, of "the liberal vision of international order," a world in which "democracy and markets flourished . . . globalization was enshrined as a progressive historical force, and ideology, nationalism and war were at a low ebb."[72] In the post–Cold War world, all the great powers were embracing liberalism, or so people wanted to believe: Russia under Boris Yeltsin; China in the midst of its economic liberalization. So the idea of an "international community" was reborn, and its task was to address the many "global issues"—disease, poverty, climate change, terrorism, ethnic conflict—on which all nations had common rather than conflicting interests.

But in the second decade of the twenty-first century, convergence feels like another idealistic illusion. The great powers do not agree on the sources of domestic legitimacy. The United States and its liberal allies naturally favor democracy. Russia and China, just as naturally, want a world that is safe for their autocracy. A new, multipolar order, were one to come into being, would include these two great-power autocracies as major players. If the history of the Concert of Europe is any guide, the lack of agreement on what constitutes legitimate government will be an obstacle to cooperation at best and a source of conflict at worst. Samuel P. Huntington, writing in 1991, speculated that if "the Soviet Union and China become democracies like the other major powers, the probability of major interstate violence will be greatly reduced." But, on the other hand, "a permanently divided world" was "likely to be a violent world." In Lincolnesque fashion, he asked, "How long can an increasingly interdependent world survive part-democratic and part-authoritarian?"[73]

Those who understand that the present liberal order was built around American power have wrestled with the question of how to preserve it if and when that power fades. John Ikenberry, among others, has argued that the task of the United States in an era of declining influence is to establish international institutions and laws that can take root and sustain the order as America declines, and to persuade rising powers that they have an interest in participating in and maintaining those institutions and those international rules. In this way, the institutions can acquire a life of their own and can constrain even powerful nations that might otherwise be inclined to disrupt the liberal order. These stronger institutions and rules would eventually become substitutes for American power.

This idea of erecting self-sustaining liberal international institutions has tantalized Americans since the nation first became a great power at the end of the nineteenth century. George Kennan and other "realists" have bemoaned the American propensity to seek succor in international laws and institutions, hoping to "suppress the chaotic and dangerous aspirations of governments" through a "system of legal rules and restraints."[74] But it is understandable that Americans would like a world order that was essentially self-regulating and self-sustaining. It is the answer to the conundrum of power and interest that so bedevils them—how to create a world conducive to American ideals and interests without requiring the costly and morally complex exercise of American power. Theodore Roosevelt thought in terms of an international consortium of great powers, working cooperatively to advance civilization—a dream shattered when those same great powers all but destroyed civilization themselves in 1914. Woodrow Wilson picked up the banner after the war, calling into being a League of Nations (in which his countrymen then refused to take part) that was meant to uphold laws and institutions backed by the collective strength of the liberal powers. The attempt was made again after World War II, with the founding of the United Nations, and again after the Cold War, when President George H. W. Bush spoke hopefully of a coming "New World Order," in which "the rule of law supplants the rule of the jungle," "nations recognize the shared responsibility for freedom and justice," and the United Nations "performs as envisioned by its founders."[75]

Many have seen the transition from American hegemony, or from any great-power arrangement, to a world of international laws and institutions as the final stage of human progress. The subordination of the individual nation-state to the collective will of all nations, the supplanting of nationalism by an international cosmopolitanism, the replication on the international scene of the legal and institutional restraints of American domestic life—these goals remain as enticing to people today as they have to generations past. The only difference is that in the past, Americans sought to erect such a world at a time when U.S. power was rising. Today, such a world is meant to compensate for an American power allegedly in decline.

Is there reason to believe we are better able to build such a world today, ostensibly in a time of decline, than we were a hundred years ago, or even fifty years ago, at a time of ascendancy? The intervening century gives little reason for optimism. All efforts to hand off the maintenance of order and security to an international body with greater authority than the nations within it, or to rely on nations to abide by international rules, regardless of their power to flout them, have failed. The new authority has proven too weak to take up the task. The nations that had responsibility and power have either ignored it or used it as an excuse for inaction themselves. The rules have generally bound only the weak, while the strong, including the United States, have felt free to ignore them and faced no punishment by the "international community." The League of Nations famously refused to respond to blatant violations of international law—the Japanese invasion of Manchuria in 1931, the Italian invasion of Ethiopia in 1935. The United States and the Soviet Union both spent most of the Cold War ignoring or seeking ways around the United Nations. As Reinhold Niebuhr observed, "the prestige of the international community" is never great enough and its individual members are never unified enough "to discipline recalcitrant nations."[76] Institutions cannot wield more power than the nations that constitute them, but they have often wielded less.

In a multipolar world, which nation or group of nations would be able to use its power alone or collectively to uphold the liberal order against those who would upset it? This is a critical question, because any order rests ultimately not on rules alone but on the power to enforce the rules. Today there is a unique situation in which the world's most powerful nation enjoys a remarkably high degree of international legitimacy when it uses force. In previous eras of multipolarity, when all nations sought security from an uneasy balance of power and operated within roughly defined spheres of influence, the use of force by any one nation outside its sphere or in areas of overlapping spheres threatened to destabilize the equilibrium. In the late nineteenth and early twentieth centuries, for example, the great powers could not bring order to the tumultuous Balkan region because the use of force by any one of the great powers threatened the interests of the others and the overall equilibrium. There was no international power to impose order. This was the dilemma Wilson attempted to solve with the League of Nations. In fact, it was solved only by American hegemony. In the late twentieth century, the United States was able to lead two interventions in the Balkans in the interest of preserving the liberal order without provoking great-power conflict. While Russians felt a bit humiliated by American dominance in a Slavic and traditionally Russian area of concern, there was never any question of war. Were the current disparity of power between the United States and other great powers to diminish, it might become impossible to intervene in similar situations without risking great-power confrontation. Which power or powers in a post-American world would be able to act with the approval of the others? The lack of legitimated military force would make it increasingly difficult to defend core principles of the liberal order against the inevitable challenges.

The lesson of the twentieth century, perhaps forgotten in the twenty-first, is that if one wants a more liberal order, there may be no substitute for powerful liberal nations to build and defend it. International order is not an evolution; it is an imposition. It is the domination of one vision over others—in this case, the domination of liberal principles of economics, domestic politics, and international relations over other, nonliberal principles. It will last only as long as those who imposed it retain the capacity to defend it. This is an uncomfortable reality for liberal internationalists. We prefer to believe that a liberal international order survives because it is right and just—and not only for us but for everyone. We prefer to imagine that the acceptance of a liberal order is voluntary or, better still, the product of natural forces, not the wielding of power. That is why the "End of History" was such an attractive thesis to many, and remains so even after it has been discredited by events. The theory of inevitable evolution means there is no requirement to impose liberal order. It will merely happen. This resolves the moral ambiguity—and the practical and financial challenges—of imposing it and defending its imposition.

There is an assumption, too, embedded in our Enlightenment worldview, that there is a necessary link between liberal order and the end of nationalism, and even of the nation itself. The rise of supranational institutions and a cosmopolitan sensibility represent progress toward a more perfect liberal order. But what if this is wrong? What if an order characterized by peace, democracy, and prosperity depends on particular nations to uphold it? The internationalist Theodore Roosevelt argued as much in 1918, in response to the supranationalist visions of his day. "Let us refuse to abolish nationalism," he said. "On the contrary, let us base a wise and practical internationalism on a sound and intense nationalism."[77] True liberal progress might be tied, paradoxically, to this atavistic concept of the nation, willing to use its power, in conjunction with other nations, to uphold an order that can only approximate but never achieve the liberal international ideal. It is when we try actually to achieve the ideal, to move beyond the nation to a post-national vision of liberal internationalism, that the whole project fails.

In this respect, the European Union may be a warning. No group of nations has ever come closer to achieving the liberal internationalist ideal, the Kantian perpetual peace. But the price has been a Europe increasingly disarming itself while the other great powers refuse to follow on its journey. Would this postmodern Europe even survive if it truly had to fend for itself in a world that did not play by its rules?

The irony is that the success of the American world order has made it possible for so many people to believe that it can be transcended, that American power may no longer be necessary to sustain it. The old dream has come to seem more real over the past two decades because the success of American power has made it seem more real. Instead of realizing that great-power conflict and competition have been suppressed, people imagine that the great powers themselves are fundamentally changing their character, that institutions, laws, and norms are taking hold. It is as if New Yorkers strolling through a safe Central Park decided that police were no longer going to be needed. The park is safe because the human race has evolved.

President Bill Clinton left office believing that the key task for America was to "create the world we would like to live in when we are no longer the world's only super-power," to prepare for "a time when we would have to share the stage."[78] It is an eminently sensible-sounding proposal. But whether it can be done is another question. For when it comes to the relations among states, and particularly in matters of power and war and peace, rules and institutions rarely survive the decline of the power or powers that erected them. Those rules and institutions are like scaffolding around a building: they don't hold the building up; the building holds them up. When American power declines, the institutions and norms American power supports will decline, too. Or, more likely, if history is a guide, they may collapse altogether as we transition into another kind of world order, or into disorder. We may discover then that the United States was essential to keeping the present world order together and that the alternative to American power was not peace and harmony but chaos and catastrophe—which is what existed before the American world order came into being.

WE CAN ALREADY SEE the signs of erosion. The number of electoral democracies peaked at 123 in 2005. Since then it has dropped slightly every year, and as of

2011 there were 115. Freedom House also reports a hollowing out of democracy, with "growing pressures on freedom of expression, including press freedom, as well as on civic activists engaged in promoting political reform and respect for human rights, including the rights of workers to organize."[79]

Liberal institutions and norms have also weakened somewhat in recent years. The European Union, aside from its economic difficulties and diminishing military power, has less moral sway in the international system than it did a decade ago. According to scholars at the European Council on Foreign Relations, for instance, the EU is suffering "a slow-motion crisis" at the United Nations, where its ability to "promote an international rule of law based on human rights and justice" is steadily declining. They attribute this chiefly to the growing influence of China, which has established at the UN "an increasingly solid coalition of general assembly votes, often mobilized in opposition to EU values such as the defense of human rights."[80]

Free-market capitalism, meanwhile, is going through one of its periodic bouts of discrediting itself. The subprime mortgage crisis and the ensuing recession have again raised doubts about the viability and desirability of the system, similar to what occurred in the 1930s and 1970s. Other models, like China's state-guided capitalism, are enjoying greater success, partly because its government's enormous surpluses have helped cushion the effects of the international downturn.

Finally, great powers are increasingly behaving in traditional great-power fashion, asserting and attempting to carve out spheres of influence in accordance with their growing power: Putin's call for a "Eurasian Union" of former Soviet states; China's claims in the South China and East China Seas; India's claims in the Indian Ocean region. They are small hints of what might be yet to come.

SO IS THE UNITED STATES IN DECLINE?

ALTHOUGH WE CAN DIMLY see the outlines of what the next world order might look like, it is still from the safe vantage point of a world order that remains shaped by the United States. The question is, how long will it last? Perhaps the mere fact that we can see the distant shore is enough to raise doubts. Is the United States in decline? And if so, is its decline inevitable, or is it still within the power of the United States, and other nations, to fend it off?

How to evaluate whether the United States is actually in a state of steady decline or whether it is going through a difficult period from which it will recover? Much of the commentary on American decline these days rests on rather loose analysis, on impressions that the United States has lost its way, that it has abandoned the virtues that made it successful in the past, that it lacks the will to address the problems it faces. Americans look at other nations whose economies are, for the moment, in better shape than their own, and which seem to have the dynamism that America once had, and they lament, as in the title of Thomas Friedman's latest book, "That used to be us."

It doesn't much help to point out that Americans have experienced this unease before, that many previous generations have also felt this sense of lost vigor and lost virtue. Even in 1788, Patrick Henry lamented the nation's fall from past glory, "when the American spirit was in its youth."

The perception of decline today is certainly understandable, given the dismal economic situation since 2008 and the nation's large fiscal deficits, which, combined with the continuing growth of the Chinese, Indian, Brazilian, Turkish, and other economies, seem to portend a significant and irreversible shift in global economic power. Some of the pessimism is also due to the belief that the United States has lost favor, and therefore influence, in much of the world, because of its various responses to the September 11 attacks. The detainment facilities at Guantánamo, the use of torture against suspected terrorists, and the widely condemned 2003 invasion of Iraq have all tarnished the American "brand" and put a dent in America's "soft power"—its ability to attract others to its point of view. There have been the difficult wars in Iraq and Afghanistan, which many argue proved the limits of military power, stretched the United States beyond its capacities, and weakened the nation at its core. Some compare the United States to the British Empire at the end of the nineteenth century, with the Iraq and Afghanistan wars serving as the equivalent of Britain's difficult and demoralizing Boer War.

With this broad perception of decline as the backdrop,

every failure of the United States to get its way in the world tends to reinforce the impression. Arabs and Israelis refuse to make peace, despite American entreaties. Iran and North Korea defy American demands that they cease their nuclear weapons programs. China refuses to let its currency rise. Ferment in the Arab world spins out of America's control. Every day, it seems, brings more evidence that the time has passed when the United States could lead the world and get others to do its bidding.

Powerful as this sense of decline may be, however, it deserves a more rigorous examination. Measuring changes in a nation's relative power is a tricky business, but there are some basic indicators: the size and influence of its economy relative to that of other powers; the degree of military power compared with potential adversaries'; the degree of political influence it wields in the international system—all of which make up what the Chinese call "comprehensive national power." And there is the matter of time. Judgments made based on only a few years' evidence are problematic. A great power's decline is the product of fundamental changes in the international distribution of various forms of power that usually occur over longer stretches of time. Great powers rarely decline suddenly. A war may bring them down, but even that is usually a symptom, and a culmination, of a longer process.

The decline of the British Empire, for instance, occurred over several decades. In 1870 the British share of global manufacturing was over 30 percent. In 1900 it was 20 percent. By 1910 it was under 15 percent—well below the rising United States, which, over the same period,

had climbed from more than 20 percent to more than
25 percent; but also less than Germany, which had lagged
far behind Britain throughout the nineteenth century
yet had caught and surpassed it in the first decade of the
twentieth century. Over the course of that period, the
British navy went from unchallenged master of the seas
to sharing control of the oceans with other, rising naval
powers. In 1883 Britain possessed more battleships than
all the other powers combined. By 1897 its dominance
had been eclipsed. British officials considered their navy
"completely outclassed" in the Western Hemisphere by
the United States, in East Asia by Japan, and even close to
home by the combined navies of Russia and France, and
that was before the threatening growth of the German
navy.[81] These were clear-cut, measurable, steady declines
in two of the most important measures of power over the
course of a half century.

Some of the arguments for America's relative decline
these days would be more potent if they had not appeared
only in the wake of the 2008 financial crisis. Just as one
swallow does not make a spring, one recession, or even
a severe economic crisis, need not mean the beginning
of the end of a great power. The United States suffered
deep and prolonged economic crises in the 1890s, the
1930s, and the 1970s. In each case, it rebounded in the following decade and actually ended up in a stronger position relative to other powers than before the crisis. The
first decade of the twentieth century, the 1940s, and the
1980s were all high points of American global power and
influence.

Less than a decade ago most observers spoke not of

America's decline but of its enduring primacy. In 2002 the historian Paul Kennedy, who in the late 1980s had written a much-discussed book on "the rise and fall of the great powers," America included, declared that never in history had there been such a great "disparity of power" as between the United States and the rest of the world.[82] John Ikenberry agreed that "no other great power" had held "such formidable advantages in military, economic, technological, cultural, or political capabilities . . . The preeminence of American power" was "unprecedented."[83] In 2004, Fareed Zakaria described the United States as enjoying a "comprehensive uni-polarity" unlike anything seen since Rome.[84] But a mere four years later, Zakaria was writing about the "post-American world," and Kennedy, again, about the inevitability of American decline. Did the fundamentals of America's relative power shift so dramatically in just a few short years?

The answer is no. Let's start with the basic indicators. In economic terms, and even despite the current years of recession and slow growth, America's position in the world has not changed. Its share of the world's GDP has held remarkably steady, not only over the past decade, but over the past four decades. In 1969 the United States produced roughly a quarter of the world's economic output. Today it still produces roughly a quarter, and it remains not only the largest but also the richest economy in the world. People are rightly mesmerized by the rise of China, India, and other Asian nations whose share of the global economy has been climbing steadily, but this has so far come almost entirely at the expense of Europe and Japan, which have had a declining share of the global economy.[85]

Optimists about China's development predict that it will overtake the United States as the largest economy in the world sometime in the next two decades. This could mean that the United States will face an increasing challenge to its economic position in the future. The sheer size of an economy, however, is not by itself a good measure of overall power within the international system. If it were, then early-nineteenth-century China, with what was then the world's largest economy, would have been the predominant power instead of the prostrate victim of smaller European nations. Even if China does reach this pinnacle again—and Chinese leaders face significant obstacles to sustaining the country's growth indefinitely—it will still remain far behind both the United States and Europe in terms of per capita GDP.

Military capacity matters, too, as early-nineteenth-century China learned and Chinese leaders know today. As Yan Xuetong recently noted, "Military strength underpins hegemony."[86] Here the United States remains unmatched. It is far and away the most powerful nation the world has ever known, and there has been no decline in America's relative military capacity—at least not yet. Americans currently spend roughly $600 billion a year on defense, more than the rest of the other great powers combined.[87] They do so, moreover, while consuming around 4 percent of GDP annually, a higher percentage than the other great powers but in historical terms lower than the 10 percent of GDP that the United States spent on defense in the mid-1950s or the 7 percent it spent in the late 1980s. The superior expenditures underestimate America's actual superiority in military capability. American land and air forces are equipped with the most advanced weaponry, are the most experienced in actual combat, and would defeat any competitor in a head-to-head battle. American naval power remains predominant in every region of the world.

By these military and economic measures, at least, the United States today is not remotely like Britain circa 1900, when that empire's relative decline began to become apparent. It is more like Britain circa 1870, when the empire was at the height of its power. It is possible to imagine a time when this might no longer be the case, but that moment has not yet arrived.

But what about the "rise of the rest"—the increasing economic clout of nations like China, India, Brazil, and Turkey? Doesn't that cut into American power and influence? The answer is, it depends. The fact that other nations in the world are enjoying periods of high growth does not mean that America's position as the predominant power is declining, or even that "the rest" are catching up in terms of overall power and influence. Brazil's share of global GDP was a little over 2 percent in 1990 and remains a little over 2 percent today. Turkey's share was under 1 percent in 1990 and is still under 1 percent today.[88] People, especially businesspeople, are naturally excited about these emerging markets, but just because a nation is an attractive investment opportunity does not mean it is also a rising great power. Wealth matters in international politics, but there is no simple correlation between economic growth and international influence. It is not clear that a richer India today, for instance, wields greater influence on the global stage than a poorer India did in the 1950s and 1960s under Nehru, when it was a leader of the Non-Aligned Movement, or that Turkey, for all the independence and flash of Prime Minister Recep Tayyip Erdogan, really wields more influence than it did a decade ago.

As for the effect of these growing economies on the position of the United States, it all depends on who is doing the growing. The problem for the British Empire at the beginning of the twentieth century was not its substantial decline relative to the United States, a generally friendly power whose interests did not fundamentally conflict with Britain's. Even in the Western Hemisphere, British trade increased as it ceded dominance to the United States. The problem was Britain's decline relative to Germany, which aimed for supremacy on the European continent, sought to compete with Britain on the high seas, and in both respects posed a threat to Britain's core security. In the case of the United States, the dramatic and rapid rise of the German and Japanese economies during the Cold War reduced American primacy in the world much more than the more recent "rise of the rest." America's share of the world's GDP, nearly 50 percent after World War II, fell to roughly 25 percent by the early 1970s, where it has remained ever since. But that "rise of the rest" did not weaken the United States. If anything, it strengthened it. Germany and Japan were and are close democratic allies, key pillars of the American world order. The growth of their economies actually shifted the balance irretrievably against the Soviet bloc and helped bring about its demise.

When gauging the impact of the growing economies of other countries today, one has to make the same kinds of calculations. Does the growth of the Brazilian economy, or of the Indian economy, diminish American global power? Both nations are friendly, and India is increasingly a strategic partner of the United States. If America's future competitor in the world is likely to be China, then a richer and more powerful India will be an asset, not a liability, to the United States. Overall, the fact that Brazil, India, Turkey, and South Africa are enjoying a period of economic growth—which may or may not last indefinitely—is either irrelevant to America's strategic position or of benefit to it. At present, only the growth of China's economy can be said to have implications for American power in the future, and only insofar as the Chinese translate enough of their growing economic strength into military strength.

If the United States is not suffering decline in these basic measures of power, isn't it simply true, nevertheless, that its influence has diminished, that it is having a harder time getting its way in the world? The almost universal assumption is that the United States has indeed lost influence. Whatever the explanation may be—American decline, the "rise of the rest," the apparent failure of the American capitalist model, the dysfunctional nature of American politics, the increasing complexity of the international system—it is broadly accepted that the United States can no longer shape the world to suit its interests and ideals as it once did. Every day seems to bring more proof, as things happen in the world that seem both contrary to American interests and beyond American control.

And, of course, it's true: the United States is not able to get what it wants much of the time. But then, it never could. Many of today's impressions about declining American influence are based on a nostalgic fallacy, that there ever was a time when the United States could shape the whole world to suit its desires, could get other nations to do what it wanted them to do, and could, as the political scientist Stephen Walt put it, "manage the politics, economics and security arrangements for nearly the entire globe."[89]

If we are to gauge America's relative position today, it is important to recognize that this image of the past is an illusion. There never was such a time. We tend to think back on the early years of the Cold War as a moment of complete American global dominance. They were nothing of the sort. The United States did accomplish extraordinary things in that era: the Marshall Plan, the NATO alliance, the United Nations, and the Bretton Woods economic system all shaped the world we know today. Yet for every great achievement in the early Cold War, there was at least one equally monumental setback.

During the Truman years, there was the triumph of the Communist Revolution in China in 1949, which American officials regarded as a disaster for U.S. interests in the region and which did indeed prove costly; if nothing else, it was a major factor in spurring North Korea to attack the South in 1950. But the United States was helpless to prevent it. As Dean Acheson summed up, "the ominous result of the civil war in China" had proved "beyond the control of the . . . United States," the product of "forces which this country tried to influence but could not."[90] When the Chinese victory was soon followed by revolts against Western control of Indochina, Acheson again observed that events "beyond our control" were "marching on the mainland of Asia."[91] A year later came the unanticipated and unprepared-for North Korean attack on South Korea, and America's intervention, which, after more than thirty-five thousand American dead and almost a hundred thousand wounded, left the situation almost exactly as it had been before the war. In 1949 there came perhaps the worst news of all: the Soviet acquisition of the atomic bomb and the end of the nuclear monopoly on which American military strategy and defense budgeting had been predicated.

A year later, NSC 68, the famous strategy document, warned of the growing gap between America's military strength and its global strategic commitments. If current trends continued, it declared, the result would be "a serious decline in the strength of the free world relative to the Soviet Union and its satellites." The "integrity and vitality of our system," the document stated, was "in greater jeopardy than ever before in our history."[92] Douglas MacArthur, giving the keynote address at the Republican National Convention in 1952, lamented the "alarming change in the balance of world power," "the rising burden of our fiscal commitments," the ascendant power of the Soviet Union, "and our own relative decline."[93]

Both the outgoing Truman administration and the incoming Eisenhower administration believed it was Soviet strategy to "break the economy of the United States" by forcing it to spend too much on defense, and both feared it would succeed.[94] In 1957, the Gaither Com-

mission reported that the Russian economy was growing at a much faster pace than that of the United States
and that by 1959 Russia would be able to hit American
soil with one hundred intercontinental ballistic missiles,
prompting Sam Rayburn, the Speaker of the House, to
ask, "What good are a sound economy and a balanced
budget if we lose our national lives and Russian rubles
become the coin of the land?"[95]

Nor was the United States always able to persuade
others, even its closest allies, to do what it wanted, or to
refrain from doing what it didn't want. In 1949 Acheson
tried and failed to prevent European allies, including
the British, from recognizing Communist China. In 1954
the Eisenhower administration failed to get its way at the
Geneva Conference on Vietnam and refused to sign the
final accords. Two years later it tried to prevent the British, the French, and the Israelis from invading Egypt over
the closure of the Suez Canal, only to see them launch
an invasion without so much as a heads-up to Washington. When the United States confronted China over the
islands of Quemoy and Matsu, the Eisenhower administration tried and failed to get a show of support from
European allies, prompting John Foster Dulles to fear
that NATO was "beginning to fall apart."[96] By the late
1950s, Mao believed the United States was a superpower
in decline, "afraid of taking on new involvements in the
Third World and increasingly incapable of maintaining
its hegemony over the capitalist countries."[97]

But what about "soft power"? Wasn't it true, as political scientist Joseph S. Nye has argued, that the United
States used to be able to "get what it wanted in the world"

because of the "values expressed" by American culture as reflected through television, movies, and music, and because of the attractiveness of America's domestic and foreign policies? These elements of soft power made other peoples around the world want to follow the United States, "admiring its values, emulating its example, aspiring to its level of prosperity and openness."[98]

Again, the historical truth is more complicated. During the first three decades after World War II, great portions of the world did not admire the United States. They did not seek to emulate it, and they were not especially pleased at the way it conducted itself in international affairs. Yes, American media was spreading American culture, but it was spreading images that were not always flattering. In the 1950s the world could watch televised images of Joseph McCarthy and the hunt for communists in the State Department and Hollywood. American movies depicted the suffocating capitalist conformism of the new American corporate culture. Best-selling novels such as *The Ugly American* painted a picture of American bullying and boorishness. There were the battles over segregation in the 1950s and 1960s, the globally transmitted images of whites spitting at black schoolchildren and police setting their dogs on black demonstrators. (That "used to be us," too.) The racism of America was practically "ruining" the American global image, Dulles feared, especially in the so-called Third World.[99] In the late 1960s and early 1970s came the Watts riots, the assassinations of Martin Luther King Jr. and Robert Kennedy, the shootings at Kent State, and then the government-shaking scandal of Watergate. These were not the kinds of images

likely to endear the United States to the world, no matter how many Jerry Lewis and Woody Allen movies were
playing in Parisian cinemas.

Nor did much of the world find American foreign
policy especially attractive during these years. Eisenhower yearned "to get some of the people in these
down-trodden countries to like us instead of hating us,"
but CIA-orchestrated overthrows of Mohammad Mossadegh in Iran and Jacobo Árbenz in Guatemala didn't
help.[100] In 1957 demonstrators attacked the vice president's motorcade in Venezuela, shouting, "Go away,
Nixon!" "Out, dog!" "We won't forget Guatemala!"[101] In
1960, Khrushchev humiliated Eisenhower by canceling
a summit when an American spy plane was shot down
over Russia. Later that year, on his way to a "goodwill"
visit in Tokyo, Eisenhower had to turn back in mid-flight
when the Japanese government warned it could not guarantee his security against students protesting American
"imperialism."

Eisenhower's Democratic successors fared little better. John F. Kennedy and his wife were beloved for a time,
but America's glow faded after his assassination. Lyndon
Johnson's invasion of the Dominican Republic in 1965
was widely condemned not only in Latin America but
also by European allies. De Gaulle warned American officials that the United States, like "all countries that had
overwhelming power," had come "to believe that force
would solve everything" and would soon learn this was
"not the case."[102] And then, of course, came Vietnam,
with its destruction, the scenes of napalm, the My Lai
massacre, the secret incursion into Cambodia, the bomb-

ing of Hanoi, and the general perception of a Western colonialist superpower pounding a small but defiant Third World country into submission. When Johnson's vice president, Hubert Humphrey, visited West Berlin in 1967, the American cultural center was attacked, thousands of students protested American policies, and rumors swirled of assassination attempts. In 1968, when millions of Europe's youth took to the streets, they were not expressing their admiration for American culture. As one senior Johnson official put it, "The things we have to do in Vietnam and elsewhere are a heavy burden for us to bear in the Afro-Asian world as well as Europe."[103]

Nor were the great majority of nations around the world trying to emulate the American system. In the first decades of the Cold War, many were attracted to the state-controlled economies of the Soviet Union and China, which seemed to promise growth without the messy problems of democracy.[104] The economies of the Soviet bloc had growth rates as high as those in the West throughout much of this period, largely due to a state-directed surge in heavy industry.[105] According to the CIA director, Allen Dulles, many leaders in the Third World believed that the Soviet system "might have more to offer in the way of quick results than the U.S. system."[106] Dictators such as Egypt's Nasser and Indonesia's Sukarno found the state-dominated model especially attractive, but so did India's Nehru.[107]

Leaders of the emerging Non-Aligned Movement—Nehru, Nasser, Tito, Sukarno, Nkrumah—expressed little admiration for American ways. Fairly or unfairly, some of their "deeply held resentments against the exploitative policies and racism of the West" were transferred from their former colonial masters to the United States when America became the superpower. After the death of Stalin, moreover, both the Soviet Union and China engaged in hot competition to win over the Third World, taking "goodwill tours" and providing aid programs of their own. Eisenhower reflected that "the new Communist line of sweetness and light was perhaps more dangerous than their propaganda in Stalin's time."[108] The Eisenhower, Kennedy, and Johnson administrations worried constantly about the leftward tilt of all these nations and lavished development aid on them in the hope of winning hearts and minds. Yet they found the aid, while eagerly accepted, guaranteed neither allegiance nor appreciation.[109] Eisenhower frequently worried that "the peoples of the Near East and of North Africa and, to some extent, all of Asia and all of Africa, would be consolidated against the West to a degree which, I fear, could not be overcome in a generation and, perhaps, not even in a century, particularly having in mind the capacity of the Russians to make mischief."[110] One result of Third World animosity was that the United States steadily lost influence at the United Nations after 1960. Once the place where the American war in Korea was legitimized, from the 1960s until the end of the Cold War the UN General Assembly became a forum for constant expressions of anti-Americanism.[111]

In the late 1960s, Henry Kissinger despaired of the future. The "increased fragmentation of power, the greater diffusion of political activity, and the more complicated patterns of international conflict and alignment," he wrote to Nixon, had sharply reduced the capacity of both superpowers to influence "the actions of other governments."[112] And things only seemed to get more difficult as the 1970s unfolded. The United States withdrew from Vietnam in defeat, and the world watched the first-ever resignation of an American president mired in scandal. And then, perhaps as significant as all the rest, world oil prices went through the roof.

The last problem pointed to a significant new difficulty: the inability of the United States to wield influence effectively in the Middle East. Today people point to America's failure to bring Israelis and Palestinians to a negotiated settlement, or to manage the tumultuous Arab Awakening, as a sign of weakness and decline. But in 1973 the United States could not even prevent the major powers in the Middle East from engaging in all-out war. When Egypt and Syria launched their surprise attack on Israel, it was a surprise to Washington as well. The United States eventually had to go on nuclear alert to deter Soviet intervention in the conflict. The war led to the oil embargo, the establishment of OPEC as a major force in world affairs, and the sudden revelation that, as historian Daniel Yergin put it, "the United States itself was now, finally, vulnerable." The "world's foremost superpower" had been "thrown on the defensive, humiliated, by a handful of small nations." Many Americans "feared that the end of an era was at hand."[113]

In the 1970s the dramatic rise in oil prices, coupled with American economic policies during the Vietnam War, led the American economy into a severe crisis. Gross national product fell by 6 percent between 1973 and 1975.

Unemployment doubled from 4.5 percent to 9 percent.[114] The American people suffered through gas lines and the new economic phenomenon of stagflation, combining a stagnant economy with high inflation. The American economy went through three recessions between 1973 and 1982. The "energy crisis" was to Americans then what the "fiscal crisis" is today. In his first televised address to the nation, Jimmy Carter called it "the greatest challenge our country will face during our lifetimes." It was especially humiliating that the crisis was driven in part by two close American allies, the Saudi royal family and the Shah of Iran. As Carter recalled in his memoirs, the American people "deeply resented that the greatest nation on earth was being jerked around by a few desert states."[115]

The low point came in 1979, when the Shah was overthrown, the radical Islamic revolution led by Ayatollah Khomeini came to power, and fifty-two Americans were taken hostage and held for more than a year. The hostage crisis, as Yergin has observed, "transmitted a powerful message: that the shift of power in the world oil market in the 1970s was only part of a larger drama that was taking place in global politics. The United States and the West, it seemed to say, were truly in decline, on the defensive, and, it appeared, unable to do anything to protect their interests, whether economic or political." Secretary of Energy James Schlesinger declared that Americans faced "a world crisis of vaster dimensions than Churchill described half a century ago—made more ominous by the problems of oil." There was, he said, "little, if any, relief in prospect." As Carter put it, "They have us by the balls."[116]

If one wanted to make a case for American decline,

the 1970s would have been the time to do it; and many did. The United States, Kissinger believed, had evidently "passed its historic high point like so many earlier civilizations . . . [E]very civilization that has ever existed has ultimately collapsed. History is a tale of efforts that failed."[117] It was in the 1970s that the American economy lost its overwhelming primacy, when the American trade surplus began to turn into a trade deficit, when spending on entitlements and social welfare programs ballooned, when American gold and monetary reserves were depleted.

With economic difficulties came political and strategic insecurity. First came the belief that the tide of history was with the Soviet Union. Soviet leaders themselves believed the "correlation of forces" favored communism; the American defeat and withdrawal from Vietnam led Soviet officials, for the first time, to believe they might actually "win" in the long Cold War struggle. A decade later, in 1987, Paul Kennedy depicted both superpowers as suffering from "imperial overstretch" but suggested it was entirely possible that the United States would be the first to collapse, following a long historical tradition of exhausted and bankrupt empires. It had crippled itself by spending too much on defense and taking on too many far-flung global responsibilities. But within two years the Berlin Wall fell, and two years after that the Soviet Union collapsed. The decline turned out to be taking place elsewhere.

Then there was the miracle economy of Japan. A "rise of the rest" began in the late 1970s and continued over the next decade and a half, as Japan, along with the other

"Asian tigers"—South Korea, Singapore, and Taiwan—
seemed about to eclipse the United States economically.
It was not just the relative strength of its economy that
impressed observers but the apparent superiority of its
economic model. In 1989 the journalist James Fallows
argued that the Japanese state-directed economy was
plainly superior to the more laissez-faire capitalism of the
United States and was destined to surpass it.[118] Japan was
to be the next superpower. In 1992, in his best seller *Rising Sun*, Michael Crichton advised Americans to "come
to grips with the fact that Japan has become the leading
industrial nation in the world. The Japanese have the
longest lifespan. They have the highest employment, the
highest literacy, the smallest gap between rich and poor.
Their manufacturing products have the highest quality."[119] While the United States had bankrupted itself
fighting the Cold War, the Japanese had been busy taking all the marbles. As author Chalmers Johnson put it in
1995, "The Cold War is over, and Japan won."[120]

Even as Johnson typed those words, the Japanese
economy was spiraling downward into a period of stagnation from which it has still not recovered. With the
Soviet Union gone and China yet to demonstrate the
staying power of its economic boom, the United States
suddenly appeared to be the world's "sole superpower."
Yet even then it was remarkable how unsuccessful the
United States was in dealing with many serious global
problems. The Americans won the Gulf War, expanded
NATO eastward, eventually brought peace to the Balkans,
after much bloodshed, and, through most of the 1990s,
led much of the world to embrace the "Washington con-

sensus" on economics. But some of these successes began to unravel and were matched by equally significant failures. The Washington consensus began to collapse with the Asian financial crisis of 1997, where American prescriptions were widely regarded as mistaken and damaging. The United States failed to stop or even significantly retard the nuclear weapons programs of North Korea and Iran, despite repeatedly declaring its intention to do so. The sanctions regime imposed against Saddam Hussein's Iraq was both futile and, by the end of the decade, collapsing. The United States, and the world, did nothing to prevent the genocide in Rwanda, partly because a year earlier the United States had been driven out of Somalia after a failed military intervention. One of the most important endeavors of the United States in the 1990s was the effort to support a transition in post-Soviet Russia to democracy and free-market capitalism. But despite providing billions of dollars and endless amounts of advice and expertise, the United States found events in Russia to once again be beyond its control.

Nor were American leaders, even in the supposed heyday of global predominance, any more successful in solving the Israeli-Palestinian problem than they are today. Even with a booming economy and a well-liked president earnestly working to achieve a settlement, the Clinton administration came up empty-handed. As Middle East peace negotiator Aaron David Miller recounts, Bill Clinton "cared more about and invested more time and energy in Arab-Israeli peace over a longer period of time than any of his predecessors," he was admired and appreciated by both Israelis and Palestinians, yet he held "three summits within six months and fail[ed] at every one."[121] Clinton's term ended with the collapse of peace talks and the beginning of the Palestinian intifada.

Even popularity was elusive for the United States in the 1990s. In 1999, Samuel P. Huntington labeled America the "lonely superpower," widely hated across the globe for its "intrusive, interventionist, exploitative, unilateralist, hegemonic, hypocritical" behavior. The French foreign minister decried the "hyperpower" and openly yearned for a "multipolar" world in which the United States would no longer be dominant. A British diplomat told Huntington: "One reads about the world's desire for American leadership only in the United States. Everywhere else one reads about American arrogance and unilateralism."[122]

This was nonsense, of course. Contrary to the British diplomat's claim, many other countries did look to the United States for leadership, and for protection and support, in the 1990s and throughout the Cold War. The point is not that America always lacked global influence. From World War II onward, the United States was indeed the predominant power in the world. It wielded enormous influence, more than any great power since Rome, and it accomplished much.

But it was not omnipotent—far from it. If we are to gauge accurately whether the United States is currently in decline, we need to have a reasonable baseline from which to measure. To compare American influence today with a mythical past of overwhelming dominance can only mislead us. Even at its most extensive, international primacy, as Huntington observed, "means that a government is able to exercise more influence on the behavior of more actors with respect to more issues than any other government can."[123] It does not mean it can determine all other nations' behavior on all issues or even on most issues.

The ability to order other nations around is not even the best measure of successful leadership in the present world order. The conspicuous independence of some of the world's rising powers today can sometimes be more a sign of the success than the decline of American influence. For it is precisely one of the characteristics of the American world order that more nations have more freedom of action. Some of this has to do with the American style of global leadership, with its innate hesitancy and inconstancy, as well as its generally democratic approach to international diplomacy. Some of it is simply structural and intrinsic to the nature of a unipolar world order in which an "island" power exerts its influence in the world's power centers from a distance. Compared with alternative arrangements, this has increased the freedom of action for more nations.

The Cold War's bipolar order was more limiting because many nations were locked rigidly into the Western or the Soviet camp. Nations in the Non-Aligned Movement and Gaullist France spent the Cold War struggling to wriggle free from these foreign policy straitjackets. Multipolar world orders are also more constraining. Great powers need to be careful not to do anything that may appear to threaten the other great powers, lest it lead to war. Smaller powers are constrained, for each great power wants to be dominant within its own sphere of influence—that is part of the definition of a great power—and the small powers in their orbit cannot be

permitted to engage in activities that might prompt conflict between the great powers, as Serbia did in sparking
World War I. In a unipolar order, the smaller powers
enjoy greater independence because the superpower can,
if it chooses, prevent regional great powers from oppress-
ing them.

So it is not a sign of weakness if more nations have
more freedom of action in the present order. The measure
of the order's success is not whether the United States can
tell everyone what to do. It is whether the order itself—the
expansion of democracy, prosperity, and security—is
sustained. The greater freedom and independence of Brazil in foreign policy can be a sign of the order's success.
The greater freedom of Iran to build nuclear weapons can
be a harbinger of its failure.

Today the United States lacks the ability to have its
way on many issues, but this has not prevented it from
enjoying just as much success, and suffering just as much
failure, as in the past. For all the controversy, the United
States has been more successful in Iraq than it was in
Vietnam. It has been just as incapable of containing Ira-
nian nuclear ambitions as it was in the 1990s, but it has,
through the efforts of two administrations, established
a more effective global counter-proliferation network.
Its efforts to root out and destroy al-Qaeda have been
remarkably successful, especially when compared with
the failures to destroy terrorist networks and stop terrorist attacks in the 1990s—failures that culminated in
the attacks on September 11, 2001. The ability to employ
drones is an advance over the types of weaponry—cruise
missiles and air strikes—that were used to target terror-

ists and facilities in previous decades. Meanwhile, America's alliances in Europe remain healthy; it is not America's fault that Europe itself seems weaker than it once was. American alliances in Asia have arguably grown stronger over the past few years, and the United States has been able to strengthen relations with India that had previously been strained.

So the record is mixed, but it has always been mixed. There have been moments when the United States was more influential than today and moments when it was less influential. The exertion of influence has always been a struggle, which may explain why in every single decade since the end of World War II Americans have worried about their declining influence and looked nervously as other powers seemed to be rising at their expense. The difficulties in shaping the international environment in any era are immense. Few powers even attempt it, and even the strongest rarely achieve all or even most of their goals. Foreign policy is like hitting a baseball: if you fail 70 percent of the time, you go to the Hall of Fame.

The challenges today are great, and the rise of China is the most obvious of them. But they are not greater than the challenges the United States faced during the Cold War. Only in retrospect can the Cold War seem easy. Americans at the end of World War II faced a major strategic crisis. The Soviet Union, if only by virtue of its size and location, seemed to threaten vital strategic centers in Europe, the Middle East, and East Asia. In all these regions, it confronted nations devastated and prostrate from the war. To meet this challenge, the United States had to project its own power, which was great but limited, into each of those regions. It had to form alliances with local powers, some of them former enemies, and provide them with economic, political, and military assistance to help them stand on their own feet and resist Soviet pressure. In the Cold War, the Soviets wielded influence and put pressure on American interests merely by standing still, while the United States had to scramble. It is worth recalling that this strategy of "containment," now hallowed by its apparent success, struck some influential observers at the time as entirely unworkable. Walter Lippmann attacked it as "misconceived," based on "hope," conceding the "strategic initiative" to the Soviets while the United States exhausted its resources trying to establish "satellite states, puppet governments" that were weak, ineffective, and unreliable.[124]

Today, in the case of China, the situation is reversed. Although China is and will be much richer and will wield greater economic influence in the world than the Soviet Union ever did, its geostrategic position is more difficult. World War II left China in a comparatively weak position from which it has been working hard to recover ever since. Several of its neighbors are strong nations with close ties to the United States. It will have a hard time becoming a regional hegemon so long as Taiwan remains independent and strategically tied to the United States, and so long as strong regional powers such as Japan, Korea, and Australia continue to host American troops and bases. China would need at least a few allies to have any chance of pushing the United States out of its strongholds in the western Pacific, but right now it is the United States that has the allies. It is the United States that has its troops deployed in forward bases. It is the United States that currently enjoys naval predominance in the key waters and waterways through which China must trade. Altogether, China's task as a rising great power, which is to push the United States out of its present position, is much harder than America's, which is only to hold on to what it has.

Can the United States do that? In their pessimistic mood today, some Americans may doubt that it can. Indeed, they doubt whether the United States can afford to continue playing in any part of the world the predominant role that it has played in the past. Some argue that while Paul Kennedy's warning of imperial overstretch may not have been correct in 1987, it accurately describes America's current predicament. The fiscal crisis, the deadlocked political system, the various maladies of American society, including wage stagnation and income inequality, the weaknesses of the educational system, the deteriorating infrastructure—all of these are cited these days as reasons why the United States needs to retrench internationally, to pull back from some overseas commitments, to focus on "nation building at home" rather than try to keep shaping the world as it has in the past.

Again, these common assumptions require some examination. For one thing, how "overstretched" is the United States? The answer, in historical terms, is not nearly as much as people imagine. Consider the straightforward matter of the number of troops that the United States deploys overseas. To listen to the debate today, one might imagine there were more American troops committed abroad than ever before. But that is not the case. In 1953, the United States had almost 1 million troops deployed overseas—325,000 in combat in Korea and more than 600,000 stationed in Europe, Asia, and elsewhere. In 1968, it had over 1 million troops on foreign soil—537,000 in Vietnam and another half million stationed elsewhere. By contrast, in the summer of 2011, at the height of America's deployments in its two wars, there were about 200,000 troops deployed in combat in Iraq and Afghanistan combined, and another roughly 160,000 troops stationed in Europe and East Asia. Altogether, and including other forces stationed around the world, there were about 500,000 troops deployed overseas. This was lower even than the peacetime deployments of the Cold War. In 1957, for instance, there were over 750,000 troops deployed overseas. Only in the decade between the breakup of the Soviet Empire and the attacks of September 11 was the number of deployed forces overseas lower than today. The comparison is even more striking if one takes into account the growth of the American population. When the United States had 1 million troops deployed overseas in 1953, the total American population was only 160 million. Today, when there are half a million troops deployed overseas, the American population is 313 million. The country is twice as large, with half as many troops deployed as fifty years ago.

What about the financial expense? Many seem to believe that the cost of these deployments, and of the armed forces generally, is a major contributor to the soaring fiscal deficits that threaten the solvency of the national economy. But this is not the case, either. As the former budget czar Alice Rivlin has observed, the scary projections of future deficits are *not* "caused by rising defense spending," much less by spending on foreign assistance.[125] The runaway deficits projected for the coming years are mostly the result of ballooning entitlement spending. Even the most draconian cuts in the defense budget would produce annual savings of only $50 billion to $100 billion, a small fraction—between 4 and 8 percent—of the $1.5 trillion in annual deficits the United States is facing.

In 2002, when Paul Kennedy was marveling at America's ability to remain "the world's single superpower on the cheap," the United States was spending about 3.4 percent of GDP on defense. Today it is spending 4 percent, and in years to come, that is likely to head lower again—still "cheap" by historical standards. The cost of remaining the world's predominant power is not prohibitive.

If we are serious about this exercise in accounting, moreover, the costs of maintaining this position cannot be measured without considering the costs of losing it. Some of the costs of reducing the American role in the world are, of course, unquantifiable: What is it worth to Americans to live in a world dominated by democracies rather than by autocracies? But some of the potential costs could be measured, if anyone cared to try. For instance, if the decline of American military power produced an unraveling of the international economic order that American power has helped sustain; if trade routes and waterways ceased to be as secure, because the U.S. Navy was no longer able to defend them; if regional wars broke out among great powers because they were no longer constrained by the American superpower; if American allies were attacked because the United States appeared unable to come to their defense; if the generally free and open nature of the international system became less so—there would be measurable costs. And it is not too far-fetched to imagine that these costs would be far greater than the savings gained by cutting the defense and foreign aid budgets by $100 billion a year. You can save money by buying a used car without a warranty and without certain safety features, but what happens when you get into an accident? American military strength both reduces the risk of accidents, by deterring conflict, and lowers the price of those that occur, by reducing the chance of losing. These savings need to be part of the calculation, too. As a simple matter of dollars and cents, it may be a lot cheaper to preserve the current level of American involvement in the world than to reduce it.

Perhaps the greatest concern underlying the declinist mood at large in the country today is not really whether the United States can afford to continue playing its role in the world. It is whether the Americans are capable of solving any of their most pressing economic and social problems. And it is true: if the United States cannot solve its fiscal crisis, for instance, it may well face economic decline. This would have implications for its ability to sustain its military capacity, which in turn would raise questions about its ability to continue as the world's most influential power. Nor are people wrong to worry about social maladies, political gridlock, and the ability of Americans to compete with ambitious and capable peoples in rising economies all over the world. As Thomas Friedman and others have asked, can Americans do what needs to be done to compete effectively in the twenty-first-century world?

The only honest answer is, who knows? If American history is any guide, however, there is at least some reason to be hopeful. There have been many times over the past two centuries when the political system was dysfunctional, hopelessly gridlocked, and seemingly unable to find solutions to crushing national problems—from slavery and then Reconstruction, to the dislocations of industrialization at the end of the nineteenth century and the crisis of social welfare during the Great Depression, to the confusions and paranoia of the early Cold War years. Anyone who honestly recalls the 1970s, with Watergate, Vietnam, stagflation, and the energy crisis, cannot really believe the present difficulties are unrivaled. People point to polls showing Americans in despair about the future of their nation; in September 2011, only 11 percent of Americans polled were satisfied with "the way things are going." But that is not so unusual in times of economic distress. In 1992, only 14 percent were satisfied. In 1979, the number was 12 percent. Neither the magnitude of the problems nor the extent of the despair is unprecedented.

Success in the past does not guarantee success in the future. But one thing does seem clear from the historical evidence: the American system, for all its often stultifying qualities, has also shown a greater capacity to adapt and recover from difficulties than that of many other nations, including its geopolitical competitors. This undoubtedly has something to do with the relative freedom of the society, which rewards innovators, often outside the existing power structure, for producing new ways of doing things, and a relatively open political system, which allows movements to gain steam and influence the behavior of the political establishment. The American system is slow and clunky in part because the Founders designed it that way, with a federal system, checks and balances, and a written Constitution and Bill of Rights. But the system also possesses a remarkable ability to undertake changes just when the steam kettle looks about to blow its lid. There are occasional "critical elections" that allow transformations to occur, providing new political solutions to old and apparently insoluble problems. Of course, there are no guarantees: the political system could not resolve the problem of slavery without war. But on many big issues throughout their history, Americans have found a way of achieving and implementing a national consensus.[126]

When Paul Kennedy was marveling at the continuing success of the American superpower back in 2002, he noted that one of the main reasons had been the ability of Americans to overcome what had appeared to him in 1987 as an insoluble long-term economic crisis. American businessmen and politicians "reacted strongly to the debate about 'decline' by taking action: cutting costs, making companies leaner and meaner, investing in newer technologies, promoting a communications revolution, trimming government deficits, all of which helped to produce significant year-on-year advances in productivity."[127] It is possible to imagine that Americans may rise to this latest economic challenge as well.

It is also reasonable to expect that other nations will, as in the past, run into difficulties of their own. None of the nations currently enjoying economic miracles is without problems. Brazil, India, Turkey, and Russia all have bumpy histories that suggest the route ahead will not simply be one of smooth ascent. There is a real question whether the autocratic model of China, which can be so effective in making some strategic decisions about the economy in the short term, can over the long run be flexible enough to permit adaptation to a changing international economic, political, and strategic environment.

In short, it may be more than good fortune that has allowed the United States in the past to come through crises and emerge stronger and healthier than other nations while its various competitors have faltered. And it may be more than just wishful thinking to believe that it may do so again.

BUT THERE IS A danger. It is that in the meantime, while the nation continues to struggle, Americans may convince themselves that decline is indeed inevitable, or that the United States can take a time-out from its global responsibilities while it gets its own house in order. To many Americans, accepting decline may provide a welcome escape from the moral and material burdens that have weighed on them since World War II. Many may unconsciously yearn to return to the way things were in 1900, when the United States was rich, powerful, and not responsible for world order. Every presidential candidate since the end of the Cold War has promised one way or another to focus more attention at home and to lessen American involvement abroad, only to break that promise almost immediately upon taking office.

The underlying assumption of such a course is that the present world order will more or less persist without American power (or at least with much less of it), that others can pick up the slack, or simply that the benefits of the world order are permanent and require no special exertion by anyone. Unfortunately, however, the present world order is as fragile as it is unique. Preserving it has been a struggle in every decade and will remain a struggle in the decades to come. Those presidents who have come to office expecting to be able to do less have quickly faced the stark reality—often more apparent to presidents than to presidential candidates—that preserving the present world order requires constant American leadership and constant American commitment.

IT'S A WONDERFUL WORLD ORDER

IN THE END, THE decision is in the hands of Americans. Decline, as Charles Krauthammer has observed, is a choice. It is not an inevitable fate—at least not yet. In *It's a Wonderful Life*, George Bailey finds himself in a terrible crisis—a fiscal crisis, as it happens—with his bank about to be ruined and his family sent into poverty. He decides that the world would be better off without him and therefore to take his own life. But he is stopped by an angel who takes him on a Dickensian tour of what his town would have looked like had he never been born. The town, now dominated by the greedy banker, is rougher and seedier, more brutal, and also sadder. People who had been good and generous have turned nasty and selfish. Others have been ruined. Once he realizes how terrible this alternative world would be, and understands the special role he had played in making his own world what it was, he returns to his life and finds that, lo and behold, he is able to find a solution. With a little luck but also with the forces of good in the town that he had supported and encouraged, he solves his fiscal crisis and lives happily ever after.

It is, of course, a Hollywood ending. In the real world, things do not have to end well. Empires and great powers rise and fall, and the only question is when. But the when does matter. Whether the United States begins to decline over the next two decades or not for another two centuries will matter a great deal, both to Americans and to the nature of the world they live in. Perhaps if Americans had a clearer picture of what might come after the American world order, they would be more inclined to continue struggling to preserve the world they have made, or at least to ensure that changes in the system do not undermine the order from which they, and others, have so greatly benefited.

What would this require? Above all, it would mean working to shore up all three pillars—politics, economics, security—of what has made this age, with all its brutalities, a golden age for humanity. We have a tendency to separate politics, economics, and security—"ideals" from "interests," support for democracy from defense of security—but in the American world order they have all been related.

Start with the reality that a liberal world order will only be supported by liberal nations. The expectation that an authoritarian China or Russia will lend assistance in supporting democratic governance and liberal economic principles—and the two are intimately related—is folly. Americans and other liberal peoples who benefit from and support the present world order therefore have an interest in pressing for greater democratic and liberal reforms in the world's authoritarian nations, including the two great-power autocracies. This is not because it's just what Americans do, because supporting democracy is consistent with their principles and makes them feel good about themselves. The far more important reason is that the future of the liberal world order may depend on it. If it is true that the United States may eventually have to share global power with a richer and more powerful China, it will make a very big difference to the future world order whether China remains autocratic or begins to open up politically as well as economically. Would even a democratic Chinese superpower pose challenges for the United States? Of course it would. American influence would necessarily diminish relative to China's. But at least a democratic China could be more easily trusted to uphold the liberal world order in which Americans could continue to thrive. It would be more akin to the transition between British and American dominance in the twentieth century. Just as the British could safely cede power to a rising United States, and just as the United States has repeatedly tried to cede power across the Atlantic to a unifying and peaceful democratic Europe, so Americans could have an easier time ceding some power and influence across the Pacific to a rising democratic China.

More broadly, Americans also have an interest in whether the global trend is toward more democracies or whether the world begins to experience that great "reverse wave" which has yet to arrive. They have a stake in the outcome of the Arab Spring, whether it produces a new crop of democracies in a part of the world that has known mostly autocracy or whether old autocratic ways, or new theocratic ways, triumph instead.

In their economic policies, Americans need to continue promoting and strengthening the international free-trade and free-market regime. This, of course, means setting their own economy back on a course of sustainable growth. It does mean, as Friedman and others suggest, doing a better job of educating and training Americans to compete with others in an increasingly competitive international economy. It means providing a healthy environment for technological innovation. But it also means resisting protectionist temptations and using American influence, along with that of other free-trading nations, to push back against some of the tendencies of state capitalism in China and elsewhere. Here and on other issues, the United States and Europe must not give up on each other. Together the United States and Europe have more than 50 percent of global GDP. They can wield significant global influence, even in the Asian century, if they can stop indulging in schadenfreude with respect to each other and focus on upholding a free-trade, free-market international system against rising internal and external challenges.

Finally, there is the matter of American hard power. In recent years, wise heads have argued that too much emphasis has been placed on military power and not enough on soft power or on something called smart power. This is understandable, given the bad experiences of both

Iraq and Afghanistan, which have pointed up clearly the limits and costs of military power. But it is worth recalling the limits of soft power, too. It is a most difficult kind of power to wield. No American president ever enjoyed more international popularity than Woodrow Wilson when he traveled to Paris to negotiate the treaty ending World War I. He was a hero to the world, but he found his ability to shape the peace, and to establish the new League of Nations, severely limited, in no small part by the refusal of his countrymen to commit American military power to the defense of the peace. John F. Kennedy, another globally admired president, found his popularity of no use in his confrontations with Khrushchev, who, by Kennedy's own admission, "beat the hell out of me" and who may have been persuaded by his perception of Kennedy's weakness that the United States would tolerate his placing Soviet missiles in Cuba.

Soft power exists, but its influence is hard to measure and easy to overstate. People and nations may enjoy American pop music and American movies and still dislike America. It is generally true of both people and nations that whether they find someone attractive or unattractive is not the determining factor in their economic, political, and strategic behavior, especially when their core interests are involved. They like you when you are doing something that benefits them, and they don't like you when you are standing in their way. The United States, even at its most alluring, has seen its influence limited. And even at its most unattractive, it has accomplished some significant objectives, as when the Nixon administration cemented new ties with China.

What has made the United States most attractive to much of the world has not been its culture, its wisdom, or even its ideals alone. At times these have played a part; at times they have been irrelevant. More consistent has been the attraction of America's power, the manner in which it uses it, and the ends for which it has been used. What has been true since the time of Rome remains true today: there can be no world order without power to preserve it, to shape its norms, uphold its institutions, defend the sinews of its economic system, and keep the peace. Military power can be abused, wielded unwisely and ineffectively. It can be deployed to answer problems that it cannot answer or that have no answer. But it is also essential. No nation or group of nations that renounced power could expect to maintain any kind of world order. If the United States begins to look like a less reliable defender of the present order, that order will begin to unravel. People might find Americans in this weaker state very attractive indeed, but if the United States cannot help them when and where they need help the most, they will have to make other arrangements.

So Americans once again need to choose what role they want to play in the world. They hate making such a choice. If the past is any guide, they will make it with hesitation, uncertainty, and misgivings. They might well decide that the role they have been playing is too expensive. But in weighing the costs, they need to ask themselves: Is the American world order worth preserving?

Not everything can be preserved, of course. The world is always changing. Science and technology, new means of communication, transportation, and calculation, produce new patterns of human behavior and new economic configurations, as do changes in the physical environment. In the international realm, the distribution of power among nations, and between nations and non-state actors, is constantly in flux. Some nations grow richer and stronger, others grow poorer and weaker. Small groups of individuals today can do more damage to powerful nations than they could in the past. In the future new technologies may shift the balance once again against them. It is both foolish and futile to try to hold on to the past and to believe that old ways are always going to be sufficient to meet new circumstances. The world must adjust, and the United States must adjust, to the new.

We cannot be so entranced by change, however, that we fail to recognize some fundamental and enduring truths—about power, about human nature, and about the way beliefs and power interact to shape a world order. We need to be aware of history, not to cling to the past, but to understand what has been unique about our time. For all its flaws and its miseries, the world America made has been a remarkable anomaly in the history of humanity. Someday we may have no choice but to watch it drift away. Today we do have a choice.

NOTES

1. The United States and China fought each other in the Korean War, but whether poverty-stricken China, one year after emerging from civil war, qualified as a great power at that time is questionable. In 1950, when America's per capita GDP was over $9,000, China's was $614, below that of the Belgian Congo. http://www.nationmaster.com/graph/eco_gdp_per_cap_in_195-economy-gdp-per-capita-1950.

2. G. John Ikenberry, "The Future of the Liberal World Order," *Foreign Affairs*, May/June 2011, p. 58.

3. See, for instance, G. John Ikenberry, *Liberal Leviathan: The Origins, Crisis, and Transformation of the American World Order* (Princeton, N.J., 2011), chap. 1.

4. The phrase "reluctant sheriff" was coined by Richard N. Haass; see his *Reluctant Sheriff: The United States After the Cold War* (New York, 1997). The quotation is from John Kerry's acceptance speech at the 2004 Democratic National Convention.

5. Between 1898 and 1928, Americans intervened abroad with force more than two dozen times, mostly in the Western Hemisphere but once in Europe and twice in distant East Asia. Then, after a decade of relative repose, Americans fought three major wars between 1941 and 1965—World War II, the Korean War, and Vietnam—along with smaller interventions in Lebanon (1958) and the Dominican Republic (1965). The post-Vietnam hiatus lasted a little over a decade, but from 1989 to 2011 the United States deployed large numbers of combat troops or engaged in extended campaigns of aerial bombing and missile attacks on ten different occasions—Panama (1989), Somalia

(1992), Haiti (1994), Bosnia (1995–96), Kosovo (1999), Afghanistan (2001), Iraq (1991, 1998, 2003), and, most recently, Libya—an average of one significant military intervention roughly every two years.

6. Almost 80 percent of Americans believe that "under some conditions, war is necessary to obtain justice," compared with 20 percent in France, Germany, Italy, and Spain. See the polling done in recent years by Transatlantic Trends, a project sponsored by the German Marshall Fund of the United States.

7. If Dean Acheson had told the American people in 1949, when NATO was born, that American troops would still be in Europe into the twenty-first century, he would have been hounded from office.

8. Geir Lundestad, *The United States and Western Europe Since 1945: From "Empire" by Invitation to Transatlantic Drift* (Oxford, 2005), p. 35.

9. Martin Gilbert, *Churchill and America* (New York, 2008), pp. 102, 399, 245.

10. John Lewis Gaddis, *The Long Peace: Inquiries into the History of the Cold War* (Oxford, 1989), p. 65.

11. See John Lewis Gaddis, *We Now Know: Rethinking Cold War History* (Oxford, 1998), p. 49.

12. Gaddis, *Long Peace*, pp. 70, 63.

13. Gaddis, *We Now Know*, p. 43.

14. Quoted in Samuel P. Huntington, *The Third Wave: Democratization in the Late Twentieth Century* (Norman, Okla., 1993), p. 17.

15. Quoted in John Keane, *The Life and Death of Democracy* (New York, 2009), p. 573.

16. Ibid.

17. Huntington, *Third Wave*, p. 40.

18. Ibid., p. 21.

19. Samuel P. Huntington, "Will More Countries Become Democratic?," *Political Science Quarterly* 99 (Summer 1984); quoted in Larry Diamond, *The Spirit of Democracy* (New York, 2009), p. 10.

20. Huntington, *Third Wave*, p. 47.

21. Odd Arne Westad, *The Global Cold War: Third World Interventions and the Making of Our Times* (Cambridge, U.K., 2009), p. 196.

22. Diamond, *Spirit of Democracy*, p. 5.

23. Huntington, *Third Wave*, p. 98.

24. Diamond, *Spirit of Democracy*, p. 13.

25. Mike Rapport, *1848: Year of Revolution* (New York, 2009), p. 409.

26. A. J. P. Taylor, *The Course of German History* (1945; London, 2001), p. 71.

27. Rapport, *1848*, pp. 401, 402.

28. As Huntington paraphrased the findings of Jonathan Sunshine: "External influences in Europe before 1830 were fundamentally antidemocratic and hence held up democratization. Between 1830 and 1930 . . . the external environment was neutral . . . hence democratization proceeded in different countries more or less at the pace set by economic and social development." Huntington, *Third Wave,* p. 86.

29. As Huntington observed, "The absence of the United States from the process would have meant fewer and later transitions to democracy." Ibid., p. 98.

30. Robert Gilpin, *U.S. Power and the Multinational Corporation: The Political Economy of Foreign Direct Investment* (New York, 1975), p. 85.

31. Prior to the mid-nineteenth century, Britain, like other colonial powers, had preferred a mercantilist system of colonization and closed markets. The United States, from the late eighteenth to the early nineteenth century, was protectionist in an effort to nurture undeveloped industries.

32. Robert Gilpin, *War and Change in World Politics* (Cambridge, U.K., 1983), p. 139.

33. John Kenneth Galbraith, *The Affluent Society* (1958; New York, 1998), p. 1.

34. Angus Maddison, *The World Economy,* vol. 1, *A Millennial Perspective,* and vol. 2, *Historical Statistics* (Paris, 2007), 1:262 (available online at http://www.keepeek.com/Digital-Asset-Management/oecd/development/the-world-economy_9789264022621-en; accessed December 2, 2011). The figures exclude Japan.

35. Ian Bremmer, *The End of the Free Market: Who Wins the War Between States and Corporations?* (New York, 2010), p. 19.

36. Paul Collier, *The Bottom Billion: Why the Poorest Countries Are Failing and What Can Be Done About It* (Oxford, 2007), pp. 3–8.

37. Gilpin, *U.S. Power,* pp. 85, 84.

38. John Maynard Keynes, *The Economic Consequences of the Peace* (New York, 1920), pp. 10, 12.

39. Steven Pinker, "Why Is There Peace?," *Greater Good: The Science of a Meaningful Life,* April 1, 2009; http://greatergood.berkeley.edu/article/item/why_is_there_peace/. He cites the work on this subject of James Payne, Robert Wright, and Peter Singer.

40. Robert Jervis, "Theories of War in an Era of Leading-Power Peace," *American Political Science Review* 96, no. 1 (March 2002).

41. Robert Osgood, *Ideals and Self-Interest in America's Foreign Relations: The Great Transformation of the Twentieth Century* (1953; Chicago, 1964), pp. 92–94.

42. Norman Angell, *The Great Illusion: A Study of the Relation of Military Power in Nations to Their Economic and Social Advantage* (New York and London, 1910).

43. Randolph S. Churchill, *Winston Churchill: Young Statesman, 1901–1914* (Boston, 1967), pp. 101, 494.

44. Theodore Roosevelt, second annual message to Congress, December 2, 1902, quoted in Strobe Talbott, *The Great Experiment: The Story of Ancient Empires, Modern States, and the Quest for a Global Nation* (New York, 2008), p. 138; Theodore Roosevelt, first annual message to Congress, December 3, 1901, quoted in James R. Holmes, *Theodore Roosevelt and World Order: Police Power in International Relations* (Dulles, Va., 2006), p. 69.

45. According to Ivan Bloch, the "future of war" was "not fighting, but famine, not the slaying of men but the bankruptcy of nations." Donald Kagan, *On the Origins of War and the Preservation of Peace* (New York, 1996), p. 3.

46. Martin Gilbert, *The First World War: A Complete History* (New York, 2004), p. 12.

47. The war between Russia and Japan in 1904–5 somehow didn't count, since most people at the time could not conceive of a non-European power as a "great power."

48. Some would argue that the "security dilemma" held between the United States and the Soviet Union throughout much of the Cold War and gave birth to the arms race. Indeed, the concept was to some degree created to describe that situation. Yet there is reason to doubt that the dynamic of a mutual search for security producing mutual insecurity was ever really at work. As Defense Secretary Harold Brown famously noted, Soviet policy did not seem to vary in response to American actions—"When we build, they build. When we stop, they build"—but followed a different strategic logic.

49. Yan Xuetong, *Meiguo Baquan yu Zhongguo Anquan* [American hegemony and Chinese security] (Tianjin, 2000), p. 23.

50. Yan Xuetong, "How China Can Defeat America," *New York Times,* November 20, 2011.

51. This view has been best articulated by G. John Ikenberry in numerous books and essays, including, most recently, *Liberal Leviathan.*

52. Robert W. Tucker, "Alone or with Others: The Temptations of Post–Cold War Power," *Foreign Affairs,* November/December 1999.

53. For the best discussion of this geopolitical reality, see William Wohlforth, "The Stability of a Unipolar World," *International Security* 24 (Summer 1999).

54. Lundestad, *United States and Western Europe,* p. 160.

55. Yong Deng and Fei-Ling Wang, eds., *China Rising: Power and Motivation in Chinese Foreign Policy* (Lanham, Md., 2004), p. 10.

56. Andrew Nathan and Bruce Gilley, *China's New Rulers* (New York, 2003), p. 206.

57. Fei-Ling Wang, "Beijing's Incentive Structure: The Pursuit of Preservation, Prosperity, and Power," in Deng and Wang, *China Rising,* p. 22.

58. Robert J. Donovan, *Tumultuous Years: The Presidency of Harry S Truman, 1949–1953* (Columbia, Mo., 1996), p. 100.

59. Ibid., pp. 52, 51.

60. Diamond, *Spirit of Democracy,* p. 113.

61. "Never in history . . . has there been a globally dominant or rising economic power whose standard of living has been substantially lower than that of the status quo power and lower than that of many other countries." Arvind Subramanian, *Eclipse: Living in the Shadow of China's Economic Dominance* (Washington, D.C., 2011), p. 153.

62. Ibid., p. 186.

63. Bremmer, *End of the Free Market,* p. 150.

64. Ibid., p. 4.

65. Ibid., p. 61.

66. Subramanian, *Eclipse,* p. 125.

67. Bremmer, *End of the Free Market,* p. 5.

68. Robert W. Tucker, *Woodrow Wilson and the Great War: Reconsidering America's Neutrality, 1914–1917* (Charlottesville, Va., 2007), p. 53.

69. Richard N. Haass, "The Age of Nonpolarity: What Will Follow U.S. Dominance," *Foreign Affairs,* May/June 2008.

70. Mary Fulbrook, *History of Germany, 1918–2000: The Divided Nation* (1991; Malden, Mass., 2002), p. 4.

71. This is a key insight of Geoffrey Blainey's in his study of the causes of war, in which he observes that "a clear preponderance of power tended to promote peace." War is "a dispute about the measurements of power." Geoffrey Blainey, *The Causes of War* (New York, 1988), pp. 113–14.

72. G. John Ikenberry, "Liberal International Theory in the Wake of 9/11 and American Unipolarity," paper prepared for the seminar "IR Theory, Unipolarity, and September 11th—Five Years On," Norsk Utenrikspolitisk Institutt, Oslo, Norway, February 3–4, 2006.

73. Huntington, *Third Wave,* p. 29.

74. George F. Kennan, *American Diplomacy* (1951; Chicago, 1985), p. 95.

75. President George H. W. Bush, address to Congress, March 6, 1991.

76. Reinhold Niebuhr, *Moral Man and Immoral Society* (1932; New York, 1960), p. 110.

77. Holmes, *Roosevelt and World Order,* pp. 129–30.

78. Derek Chollet and James Goldgeier, *America Between the Wars* (New York, 2008), p. 318.

79. Arch Puddington, "Freedom in the World 2010: Erosion of Freedom Intensifies," Freedom House online, http://www.freedom house.org/template.cfm?page=130&year=2010.

80. "In the 1990s, the EU enjoyed up to 72% support on human rights issues in the UN General Assembly. In the last two Assembly sessions, the comparable percentages have been 48 and 55%. This decline is overshadowed by a leap in support for Chinese positions in the same votes from under 50% in the later 1990s to 74% in 2007–8. Russia has enjoyed a comparable leap in support." Richard Gowan and Franziska Brantner, "A Global Force for Human Rights? An Audit of European Power at the UN," European Council on Foreign Relations paper, September 2008.

81. Paul Kennedy, *The Rise and Fall of British Naval Mastery* (Hampshire, U.K., 1983), pp. 208–9.

82. Paul Kennedy, "The Eagle Has Landed," *Financial Times,* February 2, 2002.

83. G. John Ikenberry, ed., *America Unrivaled: The Future of the Balance of Power* (Ithaca, N.Y., 2002), p. 1.

84. Quoted in Jonathan Marcus, "America: An Empire to Rival Rome?," BBC News, January 26, 2004.

85. The U.S. share of global GDP was 28 percent in 1969; 27 percent in 1979; 27 percent in 1989; 28 percent in 1999; 27 percent in 2009. Europe's share has declined from 35 percent in 1969 to 26 percent in 2009. Asia's has gone from 13 percent in 1969 to 25 percent in 2009. But Japan's share has gone from about 18 percent in 1994 to about 9 percent. USDA Economic Research Service, *Real Historical Gross Domestic Product (GDP) Shares and Growth Rates of GDP Shares for Baseline Countries/Regions (in Percent), 1969–2010* (updated December 22, 2010); GDP table in the ERS International Macroeconomic Data Set, http://www.ers.usda.gov/Data/Macroeconomics/.

86. Yan, "How China Can Defeat America."

87. This figure does not include the deployment in Iraq, which is ending, or the combat forces in Afghanistan, which are likely to diminish steadily over the next couple of years.

88. USDA Economic Research Service, *Real Historical Gross Domestic Product (GDP) Shares and Growth Rates of GDP Shares for Baseline Countries/Regions (in Percent), 1969–2010;* GDP table in the ERS International Macroeconomic Data Set, http://www.ers.usda.gov/Data/Macroeconomics/.

89. Stephen Walt, "The End of the American Era," *National Interest,* November–December 2011.

90. Donovan, *Tumultuous Years,* p. 83.

91. Ibid., p. 141.

92. NSC 68: United States Objectives and Programs for *National Security* (April 14, 1950), *A Report to the President Pursuant to The President's Directive of January 31, 1950;* Donovan, *Tumultuous Years,* p. 160.

93. Douglas MacArthur, keynote address, Republican National Convention, July 7, 1952.

94. Donovan, *Tumultuous Years,* p. 59; Herbert Parmet, *Eisenhower and the American Crusades* (New York, 1972), p. 361.

95. Parmet, *Eisenhower,* p. 537.

96. Stephen E. Ambrose, *Eisenhower: Soldier and President* (New York, 1991), p. 484.

97. Westad, *Global Cold War,* p. 184.

98. Joseph S. Nye, *The Paradox of American Power: Why the World's Only Superpower Can't Go It Alone* (New York, 2003), p. 10.

99. Westad, *Global Cold War,* p. 135.

100. Ibid., p. 122.

101. Ibid., p. 149.

102. Ibid., p. 152.

103. Ibid.

104. Kennedy observed that people in Africa who "want a change" were "impressed by the example of the Soviet Union and the Chinese" and believed that the "Communist system holds the secrets of organizing the resources of the state in order to bring them a better life." Ibid., pp. 134–35.

105. Dulles worried that the Soviet Union's Asian neighbors had seen that nation "within a generation develop itself into a major industrial power." Peter W. Rodman, *More Precious Than Peace: The Cold War and the Struggle for the Third World* (New York, 1994), p. 69.

106. Robert J. McMahon, "Introduction: The Challenge of the Third World," in *Empire and Revolution: The United States and the Third World Since 1945,* ed. Peter L. Hahn and Mary Ann Heiss (Columbus, Ohio, 2001), p. 7.

107. Westad, *Global Cold War,* p. 93.

108. Elizabeth Cobbs Hoffman, "Decolonization, the Cold War, and the Foreign Policy of the Peace Corps," in Hahn and Heiss, *Empire and Revolution,* p. 136.

109. As Rodman observed, Third World leaders were playing both sides off against each other, seeking to get the most for themselves and their nations. They were "not judging a popularity contest or making any kind of moral judgment as to the virtue of the two superpowers." Rodman, *More Precious Than Peace,* p. 73.

110. Westad, *Global Cold War,* p. 125.

111. Ibid., p. 136.

112. Ibid., p. 196.

113. Daniel Yergin, *The Prize: The Epic Quest for Oil, Money, and Power* (1991; New York, 2008), pp. 594, 616.

114. Ibid., p. 635.

115. Ibid., p. 662.

116. Ibid., pp. 698, 701.

117. Walter Isaacson, *Kissinger: A Biography* (New York, 1992), pp. 697, 696.

118. James Fallows, "Containing Japan," *Atlantic Monthly,* May 1989, p. 40.

119. Michael Crichton, *Rising Sun* (New York, 1992), p. 349.

120. Chalmers Johnson, *Japan: Who Governs? The Rise of the Developmental State* (New York, 1995), p. 9.

121. Aaron David Miller, *The Much Too Promised Land* (New York, 2008), pp. 310–14.

122. Samuel P. Huntington, "The Lonely Superpower," *Foreign Affairs,* March/April 1999.

123. Samuel P. Huntington, "Why International Primacy Matters," *International Security* 17, no. 4 (Spring 1993).

124. Walter Lippmann, *The Cold War: A Study in U.S. Foreign Policy Since 1945* (New York, 1947), p. 47.

125. Alice Rivlin, statement at a panel discussion on the U.S. defense budget, Brookings Institution, December 22, 2010. To be clear, she has called for the defense budget to be cut because she feels all parts of the government need to pay their fair share in the search for debt reduction.

126. I had to be reminded of this point by Gary Schmitt, a presidential scholar and authority on the Founders and the workings of the U.S. government. He is based at the American Enterprise Institute.

127. Kennedy, "Eagle Has Landed."

A NOTE ABOUT THE AUTHOR

ROBERT KAGAN is a senior fellow at the Brookings Institution and a columnist for *The Washington Post*. He is also the author of *The Return of History and the End of Dreams, Dangerous Nation, Of Paradise and Power,* and *A Twilight Struggle.* Kagan served in the U.S. State Department from 1984 to 1988. He lives in Virginia with his wife and two children.

A NOTE ON THE TYPE

This book was set in Minion, a typeface produced by the Adobe Corporation specifically for the Macintosh personal computer and released in 1990. Designed by Robert Slimbach, Minion combines the classic characteristics of old style faces with the full complement of weights required for modern typesetting.

Composed by North Market Street Graphics,
Lancaster, Pennsylvania
Printed and bound by Berryville Graphics,
Berryville, Virginia
Based on a design by Virginia Tan